THE
Archive Photographs
SERIES

LUDLOW

This family photograph, taken in 1931, catches the *joi de vivre* of growing up in Ludlow. Grace Minett, whose family later kept a jewellery shop at the Butter Cross, and an older friend romp on the hills near Mary Knoll, two miles west of the town.

Compiled by
David Lloyd

First published 1995

The Chalford Publishing Company
St Mary's Mill, Chalford,
Stroud, Gloucestershire, GL6 8NX

ISBN 0 7524 0155 6

Typesetting and origination by
The Chalford Publishing Company
Printed in Great Britain by
Redwood Books, Trowbridge

Dedicated to Dorothy Arrowsmith
for her infectious enthusiasm for the history of her adopted town

Contents

Acknowledgements

This book has been produced under the auspices of Ludlow Historical Research Group. I am grateful to the Chairman, Ron Kitchener, and the Secretary, Audrey Youngman, for their interest, support and help. Several members of the group searched for and selected illustrations and drafted the text on various topics or parts of the town: Dorothy Arrowsmith (Ludford and non-conformity), Arthur Bristow (castle and parish church), Bill Brooks (indexing of pictures), Connie Brooks (Mill Street), Pamela Cornelius (schools), Barbara Davies (several topics), Ivan Hall (manufacturing), Mavis Harris (Dinham), Belle Kitchener (Broad Street), Ron Kitchener (Whitcliffe and River Teme), Phyllis Ray (Roman Catholicism and suburbs), Derek Williams (workhouse and hospitals) and Audrey Youngman (inns). A special debt is due to Phyllis Ray who checked the text prior to publication and later read and corrected the proofs.

There has been an enormous amount of community interest, much of it arising from public talks on *Old Ludlow*. Thanks are due to the following for the loan of photographs and/or much information: Neil Aikens, Pamela Angell, Tom Badlan, June and Wesley Barker, Pat Baulch, John Berry, Miriam Berry, Mary Blount, Eileen Briggs, Jo Bristow, Ken Brown, Vince Bufton, Molly Burgoyne, Donald Burmingham, John and Peggy Carter, Dennis Cartwright, John Clegg, Olive Collins, John and Merle Coxill, Eric Custance, Derek Davies, Ida Davies, Edna Detheridge, Stephen Dornan, Peter Egan, Don and Connie Faulkner, Winnie Faulkner, Harry Field, Daphne French, Leslie Fury, Janet George, Jean Gilchrist, Christina Gittoes, Isabella Goodwin, Ken Grant, Lily Hallam, Mavis Harris, Reg Harris, Muriel Harvey, Doris Hayes, Stan Hiles, Jill Howarth, Edith Hughes, Violet Humphreys, Nancy Hyde, Lottie James, Bill Jeffs, Daphne Jones, Grace Jones, Stanley Jones, Bob and Donald Keyse, Peter Klein, Florence Lloyd, Graham Willson Lloyd, John Lush, Cyril Martin, Mary Matthews, Bill Moody, Jean Morris, Jean Nicholas, John Norton M.B.E., Bill Parsonage, Harry and Jean Peachey, Doreen Pearce, Helen Pearce, Pat Perry, Fred and Rene Powell, Gerald and Jenny Price, Jack Price and family, Bill and Lilian Raiswell, Phyllis Ray, Eric and Jean Rhodes, Edith Roberts, Frank Roberts, Michael Roberts, Bob Rose, Linda Rowberry, Celia Rowlands, Joan Ryder, Father Paul Sidoli, Paul and Betty Smith, Dick and Stanton Stephens, Paul Suthern, Terry Tandler, Graham Thomas, Vera Tipping, Cyril and Joyce Town, John Uffold, Charles Underhill, Eilleen Warburton, Bill Watkins, Malcolm Weaver, June Whittle, Adrian and Janet Williams, Ben Williams, Connie Williams, Mary Williams (Ludlow), Mary Williams (Kingsland) and Ruth Woolley. The help of everyone named has been valuable but special acknowledgement must go to Bill Moody and Harry Field, who allowed me unrestricted access to their collections of Ludlow material; and to Jenny Price, Celia Rowlands, Winnie Faulkner and Don and Connie Faulkner for unstinted help with identification.

Throughout this project we have benefitted enormously from co-operation by the local press, especially *The Ludlow Advertiser* and *The South Shropshire Journal*. I am delighted to acknowledge the personal interest shown by Vince Bufton, Keith Michael and Terry Morris.

A feature of the book is the inclusion of a few works by contemporary artists and photographers. I am grateful to the following for permission to reproduce their work: Robert Milne, Dan Slater and Joy Wheeler-Phillips. Peter Bartlett, for many years Ludlow's leading professional photographer, has kindly allowed reproduction of a number of his prints, while his assistant Debbie Adams has been most helpful in arranging for the copying of many old photographs. I am also grateful for work done by Jane Norris of Athena Photography.

A number of photographs have come from public collections. For many years I have benefitted from the advice and knowledge of Tony Carr and his assistants at the Local Studies Library, Shrewsbury. I am also grateful to various staff members of South Shropshire District Council and to help from Nigel Nixon, Howard Cheese and Ann Waite at Ludlow Museum.

All the above have generously given permission to publish pictures in their holding. I also acknowledge permission given by: Arnol and Snell, Shrewsbury; The Barber Institute, Birmingham University; The Bodleian Library, Oxford; Castle Garage, Ludlow, Dilip Sarker Collection, Malvern; East Hamlet Hospital, Ludlow; Lloyds Bank, Ludlow; Old Ludlovians' Association; R.C.H.M.E.; Ludlow and District Community Association; Ludlow Festival; Ludlow Methodist Church; McCartneys Auctioners, Ludlow; Offentliche Kunstsammlung, Basel, Switzerland; St Laurence's P.C.C.; Shropshire County Council; Southampton City Art Gallery; The University of Texas.

This view from the west was taken in the 1950s by Ken Grant, a Ludlow professional photographer. It is the classic panoramic view of Ludlow, dominated by the castle in the middle distance, and the tower of the parish church beyond. To the left of the tower one can see the post-1945 housing estates built on three sides of the Wheeler playing field.

Introduction

This book is a celebration of Ludlow. When Arthur Bradley came here on a cycling holiday through the Welsh Marches in 1905, he called it unambiguously "the most beautiful and distinguished country town in England". This was not a "fervent expression of local patriotism", for Bradley "was never seriously in Ludlow till this past summer", but an objective judgement by a much travelled man, impressed by Ludlow's "combination of natural and architectural charm with...intense historical interest." Forty years later Christopher Hussey, in the first of a memorable series of articles on Ludlow in *Country Life*, came to much the same conclusion when he wrote:

For sheer visual beauty coloured by...history and substantiated in richness of architectural sequence, Ludlow stands high, perhaps first, among English towns. Others can surpass it on particular points, but few if any in this union of setting, quality and texture, each intrinsically first rate. The whole place is a national monument....

The book sets out to capture something of this quality of townscape, using a range of illustrations, from paintings by Turner, Sandy and Steer, to family snapshots by amateur photographers. In the first seven sections, Ludlow's topography is followed systematically, highlighting well known beauty spots such as Whitcliffe and the Teme valley, but also including residential suburbs such as East Hamlet and Sandpits Avenue. In the rest of the book, major themes such as "Earning a Living" and "Recreation" are covered, with a short section at the end dealing with exciting developments of the very recent past or projects planned for the near future - for no town can stand still, however beautiful, and no one involved with this book wants Ludlow to be a fossilised museum. Throughout, people are featured as prominently as the townscape, for the history of Ludlow is the story of a community, just as much as it is an architectural treasure trove.

When an old boy of Ludlow Grammar School, now a Canon of Ely Cathedral, returned to Ludlow in 1993 to speak at the annual reunion dinner, he said that he had spent the day "wallowing in nostalgia". This book enables the reader to do just that. Those of my generation, or those a little older, who yearn for the town of our youth, will enjoy flicking through its pages. We remember, very readily, the romps on Whitcliffe, the vigorous social and sporting activities, the Town Hall dances, and the uncongested streets; but we are apt to forget the unhygienic backyards, the very real poverty of parts of the town, and the sharp class divisions which persisted. Those who have come to Ludlow more recently and who are as much Ludlovians as those who grew up here will also find the book of interest, to see how we were at that time and how the town was for previous generations.

But the book has a more serious purpose than nostalgia. As the town changes, and change it must, it is important that everyone involved should be aware of the quality and indeed the uniqueness of Ludlow. The way that a town develops is an interplay between national and local forces, but we are fortunate that planning legislation now gives us some control on the way these forces shape our towns. The responsibility on local councils involved in this process is enormous but ultimately their decisions reflect public opinion. If this book helps to inform that opinion, and makes us all aware of the quality of the marvellous town in which we are privileged to live, then the effort of compiling it will have been worthwhile.

David Lloyd,
Mayor of Ludlow 1988-89
South Shropshire District Councillor 1987-93
County Councillor for Ludlow 1989-93

This view of Ludlow from the north, dated 1790, is by Rev E. Williams, Vicar of Battlefield, a clergyman who had time to paint nearly all the churches in Shropshire. Though the perspective is not always quite correct, the picture shows that the castle and parish church were the twin focal points of the historic town with the ground falling sharply to the lower land in Linney.

One
Views of Ludlow

Like good sculpture, Ludlow can be seen and enjoyed from many angles. Travellers from the south, rising over the ridge at Brimfield, or from the north east at Pedlar's Rest in Corvedale, get a first distant view of the tower of St Laurence's parish church, marking the position of Ludlow's hill within its wider valley. Coming in from the north west, along the Bromfield Road, there is a panoramic townscape of the whole ridge, crowned by the castle at one end – Giraldus called it "the noble castle of Ludlow when he came this way in 1188 – and at the other by the dome of St Peter's in Henley Road, a reminder that Ludlow today is much more than the historic medieval core, its residential suburbs having spread widely during the last century and a half.

Yet such is the wealth of scenic approaches to Ludlow, that the five pictures seen here in this section and in the introduction are from other viewpoints, beginning with a distant glimpse and finishing at Ludford Bridge, on the edge of the town itself.

Henry Peach Robinson, son of a Ludlow schoolmaster, painted this watercolour in October 1852, soon after completing his apprenticeship with Richard Jones, a Broad Street bookseller and printer. The picture, *Ludlow from the Brinks Coppice*, shows the River Teme flowing towards the town, with a walker and an angler on the bank. Later, when working in Bromsgrove, Robinson wrote in his diary that he was always thinking "of that dear home that doth so distant seem". He later became an eminent photographer, first at Leamington Spa, then in Tunbridge Wells.

A view of Ludlow from the north east, published in 1811. The artist, William Gwynn, is probably the young man sitting on the tree trunk. In the distance is Whitcliffe, common land since the thirteenth century, much of which had recently been lost to large fields enclosed by straight hedges. Hillside, a private housing estate, now covers the field in the foreground of the picture.

A view of Ludlow from Ludford Bridge published in 1824 in Thomas Gregory's *Shropshire Gazetteer*. This fine townscape can still be a delightful surprise to the unsuspecting traveller coming in from the south through the essentially rural settlement of Ludford. The massive twin towers of the Broad Gate were straight ahead, and beyond the near horizontal skyline was broken only by the soaring tower of the parish church and the tall trees which once stood just inside the Broad Gate.

Two

Whitcliffe and the River, the Castle and Dinham

Whitcliffe, the River Teme and its banks and the ruins of the castle all have a tranquillity which makes this a distinct and greatly valued part of Ludlow. This tranquillity extends to Dinham, which has long been a largely high quality residential area. For centuries, however, the castle was a place of great activity and importance, the mills along the river were the powerhouse of the town's industry, while Whitcliffe Common, by providing grazing for animals, played a vital part in Ludlow's agriculture.

This eighteenth century view from near Ludford Bridge, though drawn with some artistic licence, shows the wide expanse of Whitcliffe Common, before parts of it were sold in 1793 to pay for improvements in the town. The weirs at the foot of Lower Broad Street and Mill Street can be seen, while the four-storey building is probably the silk mill which is known to have operated in Lower Mill Street and which gave its name to Silk Mill Lane, by which it was often approached.

This Zeigler engraving of 1826 shows Whitcliffe being used as a fashionable promenade. A contemporary guidebook describes it as "a rural and healthful walk, commanding a delightful view...." On the left is the corn mill in Lower Mill Street, which had replaced the silk mill shown in the previous picture.

An 1898 painting by Philip Wilson Steer, entitled *Ludlow Walks*. Steer had been much influenced by French Impressionist painters but by the 1890s he was searching for what has been called "a kind of romantic arcadianism". Some of his inspiration for this came from the Welsh border, close to his birthplace at Birkenhead and to his art school at Gloucester.

The view westwards along the gorge of the River Teme, c.1900. Whitcliffe was still being grazed at this time, so the grass is short and the trees sparse.

In spite of the problems caused by the weirs, boating has been a popular recreation on the river. This ceremony known as "christening the boats" is taking place at the bottom of Mill Street. Dated 1905, the picture probably shows part of a regatta.

A detail of a view of Ludlow taken by Lilla Buddicom of Ticklerton Court, Eaton-under-Heywood, in the 1870s. It includes the small industrial complex which had grown up around the ancient site of the Castle Mills. The gabled building in line with the parish church was still a corn mill, while to the left are the buildings of Hodges' iron foundry.

Another 1826 engraving by Zeigler, showing on the right the cloth fulling mill built here sometime before 1230 by the manorial lord of Ludlow. Fulling is an essential step in the manufacture of broadcloth, a thick, weatherproof material which was produced in large quantities in Ludlow in the Middle Ages.

The great flood of spring 1947. The picture shows the Old Street mill occupying another ancient site. The range on the right over the mill race has since been demolished, and the building has been converted into office and residential accommodation.

Ludford Weir Mill, captured in the 1870s by Francis Bedford, a photographer of national repute. The timber framed building on the right has now been demolished. The mill here was a double mill with two leats, sometimes grinding corn and sometimes converted back to fulling.

This painting by J.M.W. Turner, composed from a sketch taken in the 1790s, shows the Dinham Bridge of that time with its wooden side rails resting on stone piers. The cattle, the dog and the reclining herdsmen provide characteristic "romantic" details.

A Ziegler engraving, dated 1826. It shows the western part of Dinham, on either side of Dinham Bridge, which had been rebuilt in 1823. The people in the foreground are enjoying the walks and open spaces on Whitcliffe Common, as their successors do today.

A frontal view of the Clive almshouses, the gable end of which can be seen on the left of the Zeigler engraving. The almshouses were built before 1811 by the Earl of Powis and restored in the 1850's in memory of his nephew, Robert Henry Clive of Oakly Park.

Dinham Bridge in the 1940s, photographed by Mavis Harris, now a member of Ludlow Historical Research Group. It shows the continuing popularity of Dinham for walks and recreation. Dinham Chapel and Dinham Lodge can be seen at the top of the steep slope on the right.

This late nineteenth century view from Whitcliffe shows the gardens and houses of Dinham, clustered on rising land east of the castle. Much of the foreground is occupied by the gardens of John Collier, nurseryman. They were later operated by the Carter family.

This detail of an engraving made in 1719 shows two large houses. The one labelled "K" is the central part of Dinham House, which was built in 1719, with its four prominent external stacks. These became internal features when the house was extended in 1748. In the foreground is an earlier house and outbuilding, later replaced by Dinham Lodge. The ruin marked "I" is St Thomas's Chapel.

This fine aerial view of the castle and the eastern, upper part of Dinham was taken by Peter Bartlett, now Ludlow's leading professional photographer. The curve plan of Dinham reflects the shape of the castle's outer bailey which was superimposed on the earlier rectilinear street plan in the late twelfth century.

Another large house is Dinham Hall, built in stone in 1790 by Richard Nash, agent to the Knights, rich local ironmasters. From 1894 until the 1970s Dinham Hall was the boarding house of Ludlow Grammar School. It is now a high quality hotel.

This 1902 painting, by an unknown artist, catches the serenity of this part of Dinham, facing towards the Castle gardens. The stable to the left of the timber framed house, No. 2, was replaced by a house soon after the painting was done.

The two small cottages on the left, once Nos. 3 and 4, were tucked in behind No. 2 Dinham. They typify the tight back building which occurred behind many Ludlow frontages in the late eighteenth and early nineteenth centuries. The cottages have now been demolished.

Ludlow castle was a medieval baronial stronghold and later the headquarters of the Council of the Marches, making Ludlow virtually the capital of Wales in the sixteenth and seventeenth centuries. The inner bailey, congested with buildings, contrasts with the spacious outer bailey. The walks round the castle were laid out as a fashionable promenade in the eighteenth century.

After the Council of the Marches was dissolved in 1689, the castle quickly became a picturesque ruin. It was visited by tourists, as shown here in this 1855 engraving of the inner bailey. On the left is the Norman round nave of the chapel of St Mary Magdalene. Ahead are the Tudor Judges' Lodgings and to their right the imposing gatehouse keep.

A scene from the 1934 Shropshire Historical Pageant, showing the betrayal of Caractacus to the Romans. This was a spectacular event held to mark the tercentenary of the first performance of Milton's *Comus* at Ludlow Castle. Many local people took part helping, for example, to form the crowd of Silures and Brigantes seen above.

The success of the Pageant and later castle productions led to the start of the Ludlow Festival in 1960, held for a fortnight each summer and centred on a Shakespeare play. The stage is set in front of the fine domestic range in the inner bailey. The austere set for this 1976 *Hamlet* was praised as "an ingenious extension of the physical characteristics of the castle itself".

Three

The Historic High Street Market Place

The 12th century High Street market place ran eastwards from the castle as far as what is now the Bull Ring. Here it met the earlier north-south routeway now followed by Corve Street and Old Street. The original High Street was 115ft 6in (seven perches) wide but the eastern part has been colonised by later buildings. The contrast between different parts of the original High Street is noted by Nicholas Pevsner in the 1958 Shropshire *volume of the* Buildings of England *series:*

> Aesthetically speaking it was a blessing that the old High Street was filled in by later medieval building. The town, as one wanders through it, has now a narrow and a spacious part...a part where the eye looks unimpeded along wide streets...and another part with lanes and arches and close backyards. Both are needed in a town, and may Ludlow never decide to pull down its tortuous centre to please the...motorist or the...tourist.

The old High Street is still the commercial spine of the town, though in recent years a new shopping complex has begun to develop further east. Near the castle, however, the character of the street has long been residential, causing the poet Thomas Churchyard to write in 1587:

> On every side thereof fayre houses are,
> That makes a shew, to please both mynd and eye.

A view from Castle Gardens in the late 1940s. It shows country buses parked in Castle Square, where the High Street market place retains its original width. The lower part of Castle Lodge, on the right, was built in the 1570s for Thomas Sackford, an official of the Council of the Marches.

This view of the south side of Castle Street was taken before 1895, when the stucco was stripped from Castle Lodge. Beyond can be seen the Assembly Rooms; a three bay Georgian house, then the offices of Southern & Mountford, solicitors; and the shops of Thomas Collings, baker, and Frederick Smith, chemist. The four-storey building beyond had been an ironmonger's shop on the ground floor for many years.

Part of the south side of Castle Street in the late 1920s. The Kodak sign hangs on Beesons, then a chemist's shop, now the premises of Castle Bookshop. To the right was the bakery of Davies and Brown, now that of S.C. Price & Sons. The gentleman on the left, in front of the shop of G.A. Rix, grocer, is Lloyd the lamplighter.

Part of the north side of Castle Street in the early 1880s, taken from a photograph by Benjamin Stone of Birmingham. The properties to the right of the trees and railings are the George Inn and the shops of William Bright, butcher, and Walter Hobday, outfitter. The premises of the latter were rebuilt just after 1900 and now accommodate the Job Centre.

From the sixteenth century or earlier the centre of Castle Street was occupied by a public building. In 1702 an earlier building was replaced by a new Market Hall, the open, lower part of which was used for retailing. "The long room" on the first floor was used for assemblies and balls, whilst the Corporation met in a small chamber.

Through 1888 and 1889, with much civic pride and celebration, the Market Hall was replaced by a new Town Hall. Though stigmatised on architectural grounds as "Ludlow's bad luck", the building was a spacious venue for public events, while the room overlooking Castle Square served as a dignified Council chamber.

In 1986, amidst controversy, the Town Hall was demolished "for structural reasons" by South Shropshire District Council, who had taken charge of the building some years previously. The widespread public anger helped to motivate the refurbishment of the Assembly Rooms a few years later.

All local authorities agreed that Castle Square should remain an open space, and after widespread public consultation a scheme of enhancement is now in preparation. The street market, operated by Ludlow Town Council, helps to maintain the economic vitality of this part of Ludlow.

This photograph shows the eastern end of Castle Street, popularly known as "Post Office Square", after the Post Office moved into No. 6 (later Broadhursts) just before 1900. To the right are the ends of "the rows", the successors of the lines of stalls which colonised this part of the market place in the Middle Ages. The rows separate four parallel streets.

The widest of the streets is High Street, seen here in the 1940s. The narrow shop frontages on each side are the legacy of the small stalls of the Middle Ages, while ahead is the top of Broad Street, a wedge of buildings protruding into another part of the original market place. The boy with the basket trolley is Eric Butcher, who worked for Ernest Price, baker, at No. 9.

View towards the Town Hall, c.1900, showing the many small shops in "the Rows" on either side of High Street. Lacking floor space and back yards, these premises all had cellars and three or more other stories. The shops can be identified from Kelly's 1900 *Shropshire Trade Directory*.

From right to left in the picture, High Street (north side):

1/la Arthur Bessell, glass, china and earthenware

2 Charles Cobbin, newsagent and stationer

3 John Harper, hairdresser and umbrella repairer

4 William Webb, boot and shoemaker

5 Joseph Bessell, tailor, hatter, breeches maker

6/7 Francis Joseph Bell, clothier and outfitter

High Street (south side):

8 E.W. Harding, linen, woollen and fancy draper

9 Steward brothers, provision merchants

10 Benjamin Williams, draper and clothier

11 Singer Manufacturing Co.

12 George Collins, baker and corn dealer

13 Bond & Co., boot makers

14 Benjamin Raymond, tailor and hatter

15 Edwin Sanders, refreshment rooms

16/17 E.W. & W. Phillips, tailors (Shrewsbury)

The three narrow streets parallel to High Street have all inspired pictures by twentieth century artists, as illustrated on this and the page opposite. The recent painting of Church Street (above) is by local artist, Dan Slater. The jettied buildings give the street an historic feel while recent pedestrianisation allows shoppers to move about freely, chat in small groups and consult local guidebooks.

The next narrow street is Harp Lane, which once separated the stalls of the medieval butchers' shambles. This reproduction is from a work painted in the 1980s by Robert Milne, a local artist known for the accuracy of his detail. The street takes its name from the former Harp Inn, at the end on the left.

)n the far south of "the Rows", beyond
-ligh Street, is Market Street, between
he edge of the original High Street on
he right and the former Baron's Row on
he left, another line of medieval infill.
This painting, made in 1934, was by
.eslie Ward, a highly regarded
treetscape artist from Bournemouth.

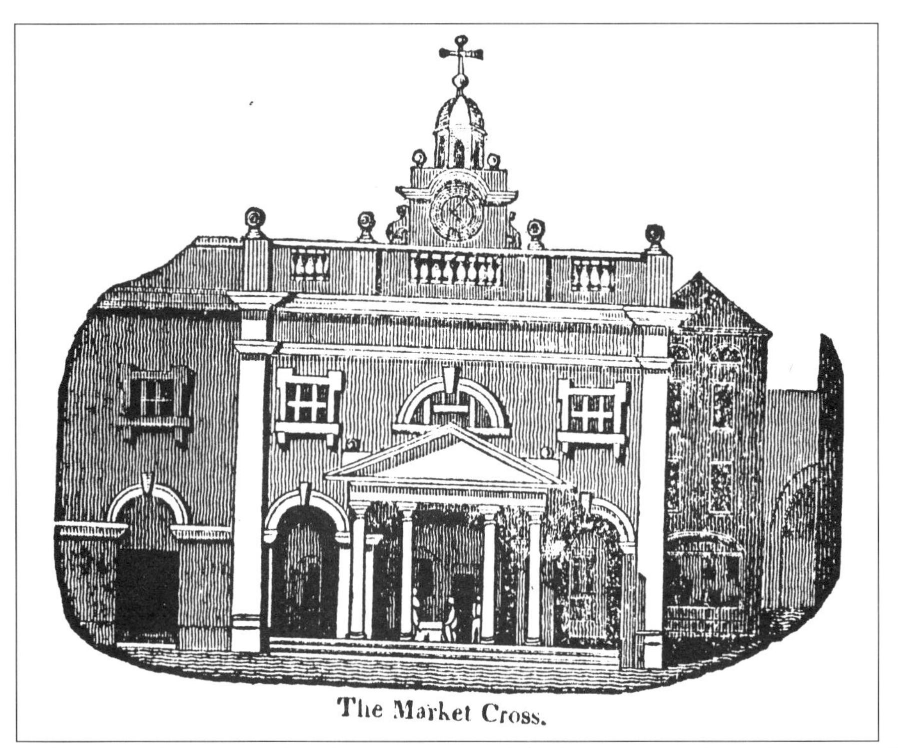

The Market Cross.

This woodcut of 1826 is the earliest known picture of the Butter Cross. It was built in 1743 by the Borough Corporation, replacing the earlier timber-framed New House. It has been much praised by architectural critics. In 1945 Christopher Hussey described it as a "richly-wrought little stone jewel", while in 1976 Alec Clifton Taylor called it "a great ornament to the town".

The Butter Cross is the traditional hub of the town. Butter and other dairy products were once sold here on market days and the steps are a favourite venue for charity efforts, such as this flower stall on Alexandra Day in May 1929.

The Mayor, Ralph Gill, and others greet Don Faulkner at the Butter Cross in 1980 on his return from a sponsored cycle ride around England. This raised £4,000 towards the restoration of the parish church Snetzler organ, for which over £50,000 was eventually obtained by public efforts and subscription.

This photograph was taken in the 1860s by Francis Bedford. To the right of the Butter Cross the south porch of the parish church can be seen through a narrow passage which once contained the church "scallens" - a lychgate with a small room above where the sexton lived. The jettied buildings on the right, Nos. 1 and 2 Broad Street, were still plastered. At No. 2 the sign of William Taylor, baker, is just legible.

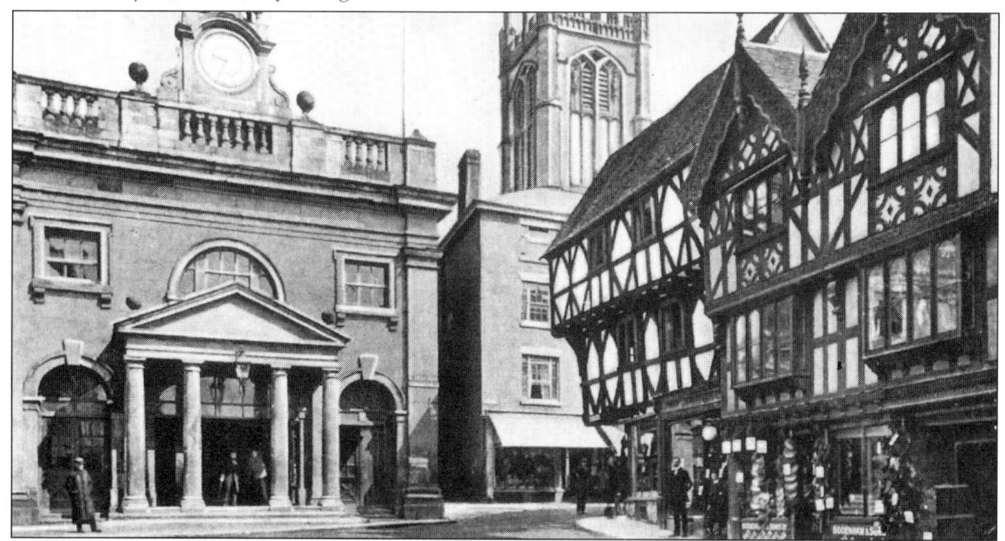

One of a series of local views published from 1916 by James Laver, tobacconist, of No. 11 High Street. The picture illustrates how the Butter Cross synchronises with its neighbours, even though its architectural style is so different. The timber-framing has been exposed at Nos. 1 and 2 Broad Street, both of which had been occupied for many years by Bodenham & Sons Ltd, drapers and outfitters.

This recent sketch by local resident Derek Davies shows the Church Inn, tucked in behind the Butter Cross on what was once a corner of the churchyard. Formerly called The Cross Keys, there has been an inn on this site since the Middle Ages. Thirsty choristers, clergy and worshippers still convene here after church services.

The churchyard has a spaciousness and a serenity which contrast with the bustle of the nearby High Street market place, both being part of a single twelfth century act of town planning. This 1870s photograph by Francis Bedford shows the parish church from the north, with a few tomb chests and gravestones still in position. The Reader's House and the adjoining property can be glimpsed through the trees on the left.

The Reader's House and adjoining houses in Church Walk, 1911. The Readers's House has medieval parts, but the timber-framed porch was added in 1616. In the 1940s and 1950s the house to the left accommodated Teff's Cafe, a popular meeting place for Grammar School boys and High School girls.

A view of College Street in the early 1980s, taken from the western side of the churchyard. The street derives its name from the medieval College of the Palmers Guild, where priests lived in a courtyard house. In 1884 the building was converted into a cottage hospital, shown in the centre of this picture. This closed in 1982. It is now part of College Court, a sheltered housing complex. Hosier's Almshouses can be seen on the far left and part of the rectory on the right.

A sketch of the rectory by an unknown artist, 1842. The central cross-wing and the right-hand range have an early fourteenth century roof and probably constitute the oldest domestic building in Ludlow. The large window on the right gave light to the hall/main living area, whilst below was an undercroft, now the rector's study, with a modern window through the three foot thick wall.

This aerial view shows the dense concentration of buildings in this part of Ludlow. The end of all three infilling rows can be seen at the foot of the picture, where the main thoroughfare twists from modern High Street into King Street. The rectangle of buildings to the right of King Street is a wedge pushed into the historic High Street from the south. The buildings to the left of King Street encroach on to the churchyard, their owners paying fees for this into the eighteenth century. Towards the top right hand corner of the picture King Street widens into the triangular Bull Ring, on the far side of which properties have buildings reaching back to the town wall. The picture also shows the cruciform plan and noble proportions of St Laurence's parish church, most of which was rebuilt in the mid-fifteenth century in the soaring perpendicular style of the day.

The wider, western end of King Street, seen through the gap between the Butter Cross and Bodenhams. The photograph was taken between 1889, when Barclays Bank (left of centre) was built, and 1913, when Bodenhams was stripped of its plaster. To the right of Barclays bank were the premises of James Evans & Sons, drapers since the 1860s. Next are the premises of Bessell & Son, also drapers since the 1860s. In the early 1920s Bessells were bought out by Evans', to create Ludlow's largest shop, with tea rooms on the first floor.

Looking westwards along King Street towards the Butter Cross in the late 1940s, at the point where the street is called "the Narrows". The shop on the right, with the recessed entrance, is the London Tea Company, which sold china and earthenware. One of the schoolgirls outside that shop is Jenny Shephard, now Jenny Vaughan, an active member of Festive Ludlow and Ludlow Festival Council.

Looking east along King Street to the Bull Ring in the early 1880s. On the left is Kingston Place, a medieval complex of five shops with solars above which was rebuilt in 1576. The two shops on the left, then occupied by a bootseller and a poulterer, are still standing, but in 1884 the other three shops were replaced by the premises of Gaius Smith, grocer.

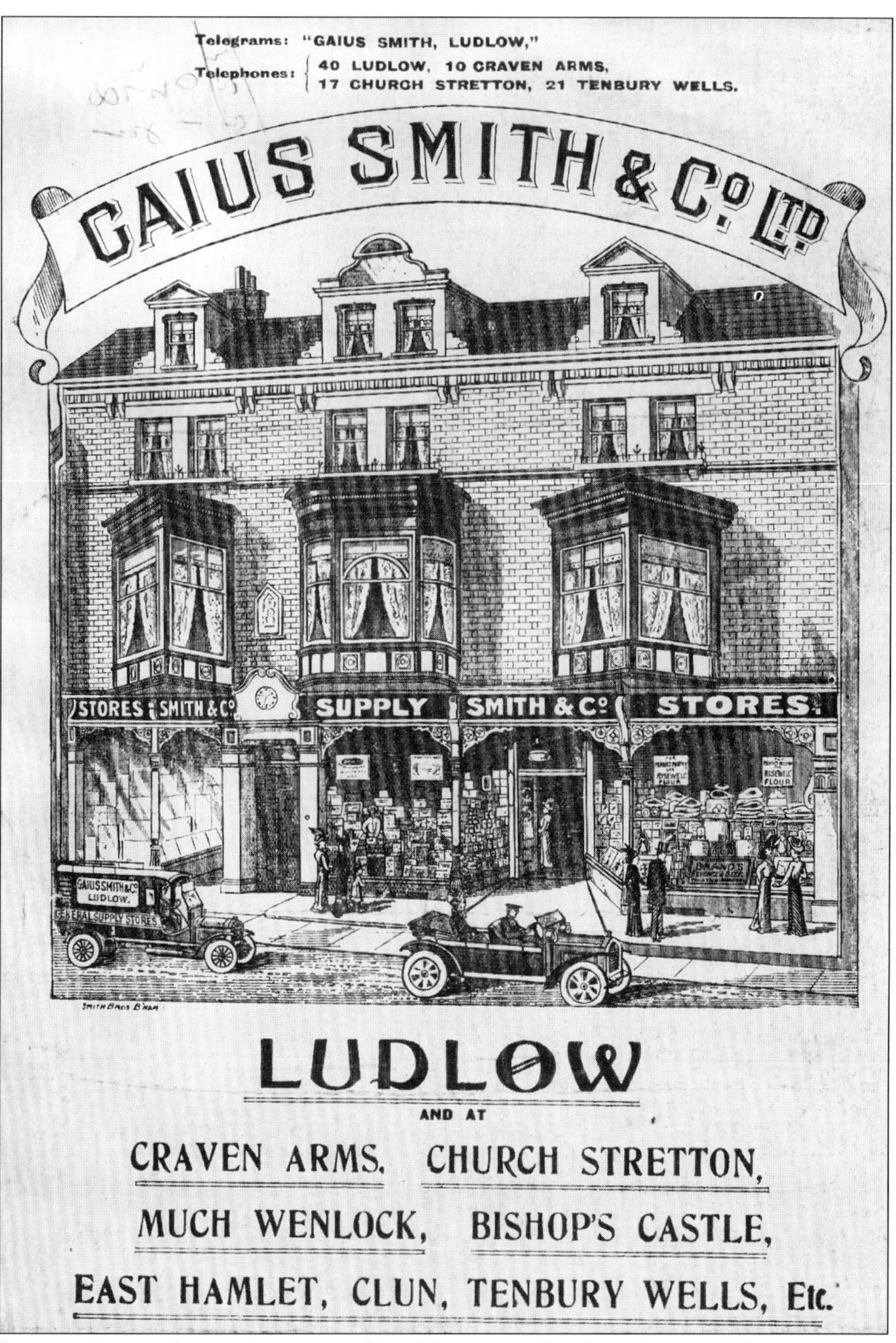

This paper bag, with pencil jottings still visible, gives a fine frontal view of the new premises erected by Gaius Smith, though the diminutive vehicles and pedestrians clearly exaggerate the size of the business. The building sadly lost much of its character when it was gutted and re-fronted in the late 1960s to form Pearl Assurance House.

This photograph taken in the early 1920s shows "the Narrows" beginning to open out into the triangular Bull Ring, formerly called "the Beaste Market". On the left, occupying what was once the Bear Inn, is the shop of George Woodhouse & Son, chemists and druggists, which later became Boots the Chemists.

From an early date the Bull Ring was colonised by two island blocks of building. These can be seen on this 1950s photograph taken from near the junction with King Street. One of the blocks, the Tolsey, is in the centre of the picture. The other, just visible on the left, was known until this century as "the Shelde", a derivation from the Latin "selda" meaning stalls.

The paved passage between the Shelde, on the right, and the shops on the left, which back on to the churchyard, 1967. The shops of two multiple firms dominate the picture: on the right, Ross and Sons, Ltd, boot and shoe retailers throughout the Welsh Marches; and Currys on the left. Beyond can be seen the sign of Stuart's cafe, established by G. Stuart-Page in the 1930s.

This photograph from the National Monuments Record, taken about 1960, shows the Tolsey and "the Shelde" from the south. The plaster was stripped from the Tolsey soon afterwards. On the right are the premises of Rickards & Sons, ironmongers, established in 1864 and still trading in 1995.

This postcard, published c.1910, shows the north-east part of the Bull Ring, which is aligned with Corve Street and Old Street along the north-south prehistoric routeway through the town. A corner of the Shelde is on the left. On the far right is the shop of J. Grant, tobacconist, and then the King's Head, with its prominent sign boards.

This indistinct but important photograph, taken in the early 1870's, gives the only known view of the timber framed building at No. 8 Bull Ring, the site now occupied by an extension of the Midland Bank. It was occupied by Samuel John Davies, baker.

This family photograph, dated 1916, was taken behind the King's Head, one of many such backyards in the crowded town centre. The man on the horse is John Fury, hairdresser, a Boer War veteran, who may have been helping to enlist troops for the First World War. He lived in the house on the left, part of No. 4 Tower Street, now a wallpaper shop.

The best known building in the Bull Ring is the Feathers Hotel, of which was written in *The New York Times* in 1983 that "it is one of the prime images of Olde England, portrayed on posters and brochures wherever tourism is known". The above picture shows the Feathers about 1800, when it was an important posting inn. The entrance was then at the left hand end of the building and the balcony had not yet been built.

Part of an advertisement which appeared in *The New Yorker* in 1982, showing the landlord, Peter Nash, on the balcony added to the Feathers in the 1840s.

Four

Mill Street, Broad Street and Old Street, with The Lanes

The long, south-facing slope from the historic High Street to the River Teme is occupied by a rectilinear street system. Almost certainly this was laid out after the High Street itself and perhaps dates from the later twelfth century. The main streets are Mill Street, Broad Street and Old Street, but originally there were subsidiary streets between them, of which Raven Lane and St John's Lane (once called Narrow Lane and Frog Lane) are the two survivors. There are also a number of connecting cross lanes, including Bell Lane and Brand Lane, now part of the town's one way traffic system.

Old Street, as its name suggests, predates this phase of town planning, and follows the line of a prehistoric and Roman trackway. The other main streets, Broad Street and Mill Street, are exceptionally wide, perhaps because they were originally used as markets. The American novelist Henry James saw them as a sign of decayed grandeur when he visited Ludlow in the 1870s, a few years after the town's heyday as a fashionable social centre:

> Its streets are wide and clean, empty and a little grassgrown, and bordered with spacious, mildly-ornamented brick houses...the place seems to say that a hundred years ago or less it was the centre of a large, provincial society....It must have transported itself to Ludlow for the season...and there entertained itself in decent emulation of that metropolis which a choice of railway lines had not placed within its immediate reach...

No street better illustrates the elegance of Georgian Ludlow than Broad Street. This famous painting by Samuel Scott, sometimes called "the English Canaletto", shows the street in the mid-1760s, when most properties had been rebuilt or refronted. Some of the people shown can be identified, for example Alexander Stuart on the far right, a distant relative of the royal Stuarts, who divided his time between Ludlow and his estates in Scotland.

This photograph, taken between 1870 and 1890, gives a fine general view of Mill Street, climbing from the River Teme to Castle Square. The street took its name from the town's first mill site, the weir and sluice gate of which are visible. Lower Mill Street narrows at the site of Mill Gate, where two small children can be seen.

A view back down Lower Mill Street from near the site of Mill Gate, showing a range of late eighteenth century cottages. These have now been demolished although the three storey range in the middle distance remains.

An early twentieth century view of part of the west side of Mill Street. The pair of houses in the middle of the picture, each with three upper windows, had recently been built on the site of the demolished Ludlow Theatre. The small girl on the left, standing with her brother outside their house at No. 17, is Kath Oakes, well known in later life for delivering bread and cakes from Marston's Bakery.

The eastern side of Mill Street above Mill Gate. The largest building is Ludlow Grammar School. The wooden hut, built to provide extra accommodation in 1872, was replaced by a permanent classroom in 1908. The picture, published after 1895 by J.C. Austen, the Broad Street bookseller and printer, gives a glimpse of a tree further up the street, beyond Bell Lane.

A fine painting by Leslie Ward, who portrayed several parts of Ludlow in the 1930s. The building with the cupola, next to the Guildhall, was built in the 1790s by Richard Nash, to provide stabling for his large house in Dinham. The jettied cottage next door, extended at the rear and divided into two dwellings by the 1840s, contains high quality plaster work.

The east side of the upper part of Mill Street, 1960s. This is a particularly fine sequence of eighteenth century facades, though in some cases, for example the house with the antiques sign, the lack of frontal symmetry reveals an earlier interior.

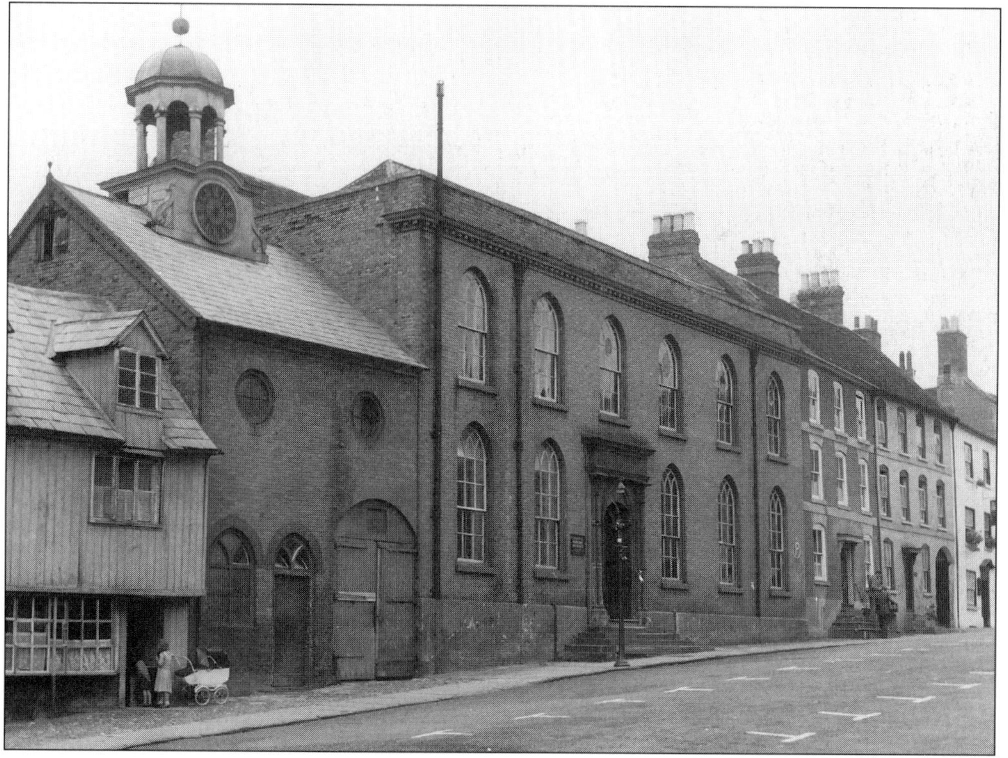

Another fine architectural sequence on the west side of Mill Street, 1952. The dominant building is the Guildhall, refronted and restored in 1768 around an early fifteenth century timber frame, when the Palmers Guild had their headquarters here. The houses on the right were built in 1713, within the old Guildhall enclosure.

The upper part of Broad Street in 1880, with large houses on either side. There are shops at the top, those on the right being under a covered way or piazza, a feature found in a number of towns in south west England but rare elsewhere. The Georgian house on the right of the picture, once the town house of the Rockes of Clungunford, was later replaced by Lloyds Bank.

This grocer's shop, illustrated on an advertisment of 1924, was at the top end of the piazza. It survived until about 1960, though the stucco was removed soon after this picture was taken. The passage at the side of the shop has recently been paved and re-opened to connect Broad Street to Old Street; it has been named Valentine's Walk.

The west side of upper Broad Street in 1967, showing cars parked on the historic cobbles. In 1960 a move was made to cover these with tarmac, causing newspaper headlines such as "Rector would Camp on Cobbles" and "Petition Organised". The cobbles were saved and are now listed as an important part of the streetscape!

A photograph by Thomas Jones of a town house once occupied by the Salweys of Richards Castle. It was built in the 1740s to a design of William Baker, architect of the Butter Cross. It later became the Crown Hotel and then a private residence. In 1879 it was replaced by the new Wesleyan Methodist church.

This early nineteenth century painting by local artist William Gwynn illustrates the vibrant life of Georgian Broad Street. A small coach pulls away from the town residence of the Boynes of Burwarton, while pedestrians greet each other and exercise their pets.

This postcard from Valentine's series, postmarked 1913, shows the same part of Broad Street about a century later, but looking the other way. The visual importance of the Broad Gate, closing the vista at this end of the street, has been stressed by many writers.

An alluring glimpse of Lower Broad Street, seen through the portcullis arch of Broad Gate, 1940s. Historically, Lower Broad Street was an artisan part of the town, with weavers, dyers and tenterers prominent in the late Middle Ages, when Ludlow's cloth making industry thrived.

Lower Broad Street in the 1880s, painted by George Phoenix, a specialist in townscapes who exhibited at the Royal Academy. On the right two draught horses are emerging from the Bell Inn, which then had stabling for thirty horses. On the left two men work the hoist at Teme Mills, where worsted cloth was produced, a late survivor of Ludlow's cloth manufacture.

The row of cottages behind No. 63 Lower Broad Street, a property known as the Vineyard, c.1900. Back building of this kind was commonplace after 1760, when Ludlow's population doubled in seventy years. The photograph was taken by Jane Green, a lady of leisure with an interest in social history.

This Walter Scott postcard from the 1950s shows most of the west side of Old Street. Though Old Street is not generally considered one of Ludlow's best streets architecturally, the houses relate well to each other and to the slope.

The Preacher's House in 1900, photographed by Jane Green. Part of the Golden Lion can be seen on the right and the entrance to the Congregational Church on the left. Two boys with a Gaius Smith's delivery barrow take the chance of a rest as they labour up the hill.

The top of the east side of Old Street in 1967, showing the former Trustees Savings Bank at No. 3, G.H. Smallwood & Co., Electrical Contractors at No. 5 and Macdonalds snack bar at No. 7. The Clifton Cinema is off picture to the right but a forthcoming feature is clearly advertised.

A procession, headed by the Mayor, Thomas Atherden, banker, and the Borough Council, coming down Old Street on 22 June 1897 as part of the Ludlow celebrations for Queen Victoria's Diamond Jubilee. The two breaks in the building line were for the site of the British School (left), opened the following year, and the Primitive Methodist Church (right).

This Valentine's postcard, published before 1909, gives a view of the graceful curve at the bottom of Old Street. This part of the town was called Holdgate Fee, due to ancient manorial rents payable to the Lord of Holdgate, a parish in Corvedale.

The centre of the block of land between Holdgate Fee and what is now St John's Lane remained a field until the whole area was redeveloped about 1970. This photograph shows the back wings, lean-to sheds and small gardens of some of the houses in Holdgate Fee.

Two of the surviving back access lanes. On the left is Raven Lane, looking towards Castle Street, with jettied houses that were once the homes of Ludlow tradesmen. On the right is St John's Lane (formerly Frog Lane), looking towards the River Teme, as it was before the redevelopment of Holdgate Fee.

The delivery van of the Shrewsbury Co-operative Society, which had a shop in Tower Street, is seen here in Bell Lane, part of the cross lane linking Mill Street, Broad Street and Old Street. The occasion is perhaps the 1937 Coronation.

Five

Corve Street, Linney and Galdeford

Of the three historic parts of north and east Ludlow, the oldest planned unit is probably Corve Street, most of which had been burgaged before 1186. But Linney and Galdeford are both ancient place names, and were probably in use even earlier. Linney, used first to describe what today is called Upper Linney, meant the dry land above the wet area where flax is grown. Galdeford perhaps relates to infertile land by the ford at the bottom of Lower Galdeford.

Medieval and early modern Corve Street was a long extra-mural suburb, stretching from the town wall at Corve Gate to an early crossing place of the River Corve at Corve Bridge. The suburb had its own lower gate, just above the place where Foxe's Almshouses were built in the 1590s. The upper section of the street became a fashionable residential area, with Georgian houses comparable to those in Broad Street, Mill Street and Dinham. The lower section had commercial and industrial premises, first for cloth manufacturing, later for malting and the leather trades.

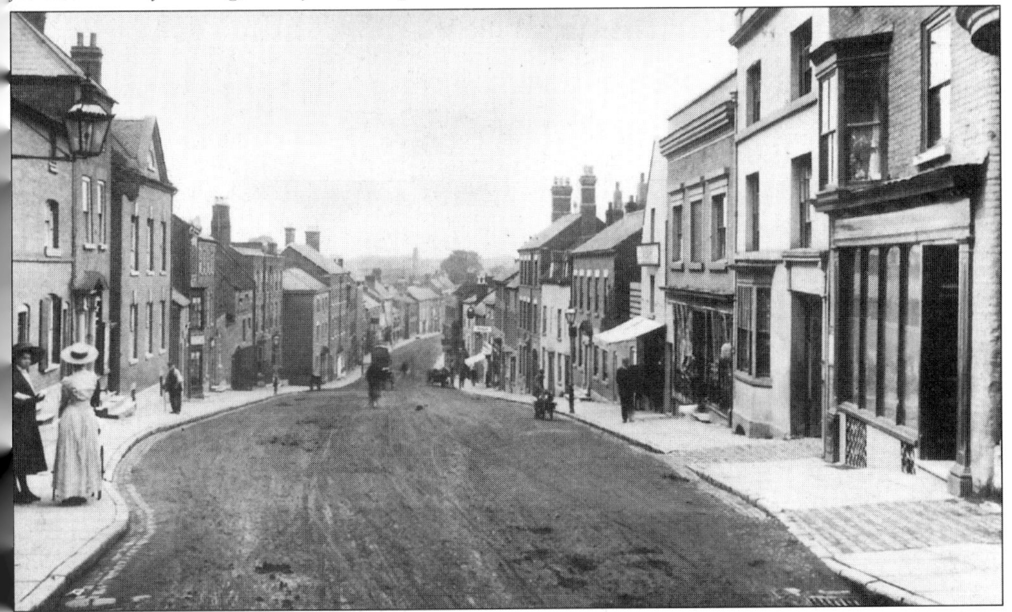

Upper Corve Street, c.1910. The great width perhaps indicates an early market function. There are a few shops on the right but large brick houses predominate. The street is almost free of traffic but the sign of the Ludlow Motor Garage, nearly at the bottom on the right, presages the fumes and congestion of later years.

Corve Street looking southwards in 1812, painted by William Gwynn, a local artist. The soaring tower of St Laurence's parish church dominates the view, as it does from many parts of the town. The two-storey building on the left, beyond the walled garden, is No. 114, probably the house where a few years later a young doctor, Henry Hickman, made important discoveries in the use of anaesthetics.

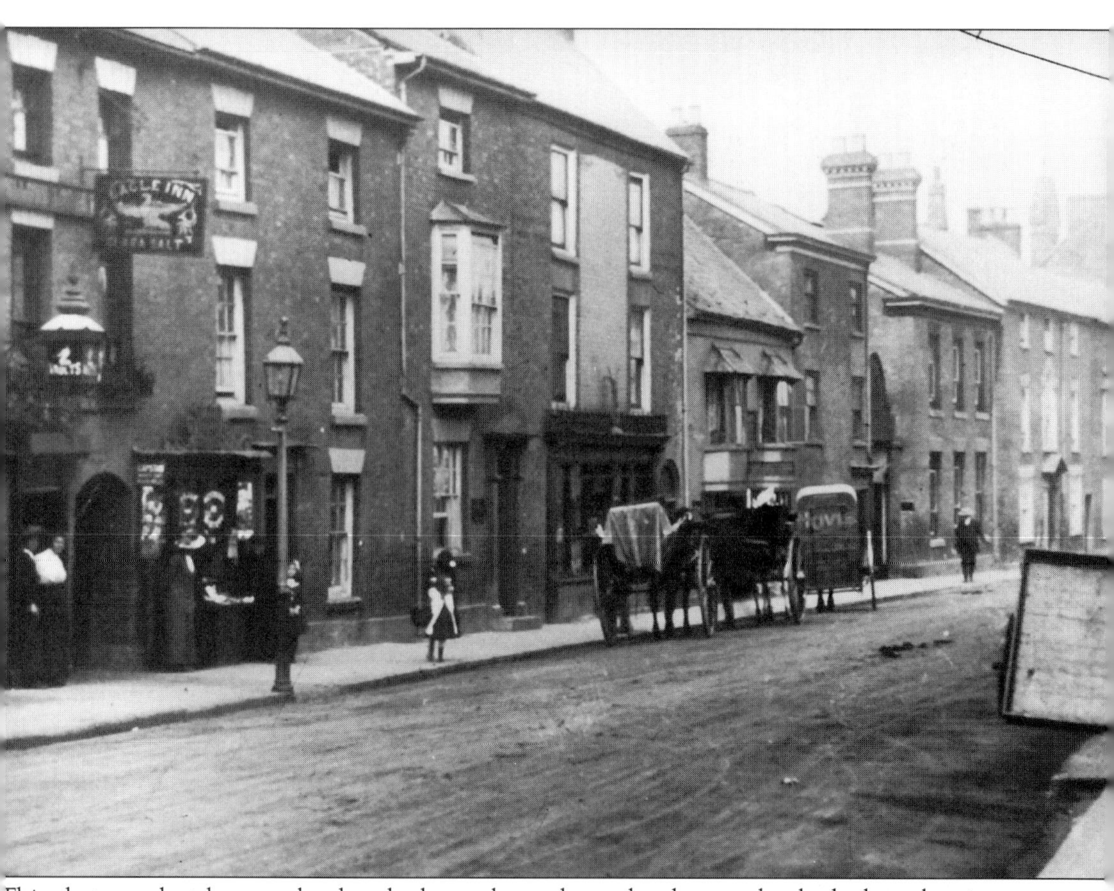

This photograph, taken nearly a hundred years later, shows the changes that had taken place in his part of Corve Street by 1909. From left to right, the occupiers of the properties were:

No.17 The Eagle Vaults Public House, landlady Mrs Clara Salt
No.19 Thomas Miller, shoeing smith (rear)
Mrs Elizabeth Miller, tobacconist (front)
No.20 Mrs T. Bennett, apartments
No.21 Mrs Morgan, furnished apartments
No.22 George Wagstaff, pork butcher
No.23 John Badger, maltster
No.24 Charles Gerrard, District Superintendent, Refuge Assurance Co. Ltd
No.25 William Blaker & Sons Ltd, coal and coke factors
No.28 Henry Lloyd, maltster
No.29 Harper & Sons, antique and curiosity shop

Nos. 23 and 24 were demolished in the late 1960s to provide a forecourt for Castle Garage.

Opposite: An enlargement from William Gwynn's painting of 1812, showing part of the west ide of Corve Street. A number of imposing Georgian houses, including Nos. 14-15 on the far eft and No. 30 on the right, are mixed with older and generally smaller properties, including he Eagle and Child Inn at No. 17, which then revealed its timber-framed facade. Some of the town's master glovers lived here, including John Jones at No. 22 and Samuel Acton, a prominent member of the Corporation, at No. 30.

The lower part of Corve Street in the 1950s. The properties on the left were a specialised industrial area. In 1724 the sites were occupied by three tanners, three glovers and three maltsters. The entrance to St Mary's Lane, branching off at an angle, can be seen on the right.

St Mary's Lane, looking back towards Corve Street. The farm building and wall on the left have been demolished to provide access to St Mary's Mews, a modern housing development. The building on the right is now the Friends Meeting House.

Flooding of the River Corve in the early 1990s as photographed by Jenny Price. The picture gives a rarely taken view of the backs of the former industrial properties in Corve Street. The tanning trade, in particular, needed large supplies of water.

Corve Bridge, in the 1920s. This was rebuilt in 1783, using stones from the demolished St Leonard's Chapel. Until Coronation Avenue was opened in 1931 – it was named six years later – all traffic coming into Ludlow from Bromfield Road crossed the river here.

This painting by G.P. Boyce, exhibited in 1872, shows the site of Linney Gate, a small postern from College Street into Linney. The house on the right, which stands in the town ditch and astride the town wall, was built in the 1770s for William Edwards, a Ludlow ironmonger. The steps lead up to a gate into the churchyard. Boyce specialised in townscapes and his work has been compared with that of the Dutch School.

Linney, a low-lying area in the north west of the historic town, in the 1940s. The rectilinear pattern of the medieval burgages is still apparent, but due to the risk of floods this area remained in largely agricultural and commercial use until after 1945. On the left, conforming to the geometrical layout, one can see the pavilion, bowling green and tennis courts of Linney Sports Club.

A view of Linney in the early 1990s, when many large houses and bungalows had been built, making this a high quality residential area.

Upper (right) and Lower (left) Galdeford converging at the site of what was once Galdeford Gate, 1967. The tower gateway (inset) was demolished in 1764 and a new prison, with an imposing if grim facade, was built on one side of the street. Next to it, on the former town ditch, was the police superintendent's house.

Tower Street in 1967, once called "Galdeford within the Gate". On the right are the premises of the Co-operative Society, which moved here in the 1930s. After fierce debate, Tower Street was pedestrianised in 1991, though with access maintained at certain times for delivery vehicles.

A view along Upper Galdeford towards the triangular open space outside the former Galdeford Gate. The terraced houses and other buildings on the right mostly date from the early nineteenth century, when there was intensive development in this part of Ludlow.

A photograph taken from the church tower in 1962 by Reg Harris, a skilled amateur photographer, reveals the congested back building behind the fronts shown on the previous picture. Portcullis Lane ran behind the long barn with the curved roof.

Further along Upper Galdeford, with Passey's grocery and greengrocery shop at the far end of the terrace. The building with railings was once the Greyhound Inn. Station Drive now joins Gravel Hill close to this point.

The New Inn on the opposite side of Upper Galdeford, c.1920. The tall warehouse just visible on the right was at the entrance to the former pound, where stray animals were kept. By the 1920s it had become a small depot for Borough Council workmen.

Beard's shop, established here about 1910, was for many years a familiar feature on the busy corner between Upper and Lower Galdeford. On the left can be seen the offices of *The Ludlow Advertiser*, which replaced the Birmingham Arms in 1914.

These buildings on the north side of Lower Galdeford were demolished in 1967, to make room for new council houses. The ornate building in the centre was the front block of what had been the tannery of William Gardener in the late nineteenth century.

The jumble of houses still to be found in this and other parts of Ludlow is well illustrated here by a contemporary local artist, Joy Wheeler-Phillips. A line of back buildings can be seen in the middle of the picture, behind a larger building with its roof line parallel to the street.

This family snapshot, taken in 1945, shows three Ludlow ladies Edith Peachey (left), Lily Hallam (centre) and Flo Bytheway (right) standing in Warrington Gardens, a long row of terraced houses at right angles to Lower Galdeford.

Six
Ludford

Ludford is an ancient nucleated settlement but proximity to Ludlow has made it effectively the town's oldest suburb. John Leland described it as "Luddeford suburbe" when he passed through on his way into Ludlow in 1540. With its large manor house, ancient church and a number of other large and small buildings, Ludford is a near perfect historic village, which adds much to the beauty and interest of Ludlow.

These boys have chosen a vantage point on Whitcliffe for a serious discussion of male affairs! The boy on the back row (left) is Oscar Watkins, from a well known Ludlow business family. The view includes the medieval Ludford Bridge, while the roof tops of the village of Ludford can be seen on the right. The picture was found by a Ludlovian in a bookshop in the USA.

An early nineteenth century drawing by Edward Hodson junior showing the parish church of St Giles and the adjacent churchyard. To the side are the gables of Ludford House with its detached summerhouse. The tranquillity seems to have been broken by the intrusion of a pig, which a boy is seeking to remove.

Ludford House is a large manor house, with a long and complex architectural history. This "Peacock Series" postcard shows the front of the house, seen from the churchyard. The hall range and porch are straight ahead, with the solar wing on the left.

This picture comes from a scrapbook compiled by the Rev Charles Kent, a mid-nineteenth century Vicar of Ludford. A gardener is trimming the lawn while a small group relaxes in the foreground. Behind is the long garden range, which was remodelled in the mid-eighteenth century.

The former service range of Ludford House, c.1905. The repetitive pattern of the four huge chimney stacks suggests a building once used for communal living. It is known that the thirteenth century Leper Hospital of St Giles, later converted into an almshouse, was in the vicinity.

After Ludford House, the grandest residence in Ludford was that built in the early seventeenth century by Humphrey Powell, an official of the Council of the Marches. It later became the Bell Inn, and was then converted into two dwellings, as shown on this late nineteenth century postcard. The house was restored as a single dwelling in 1910.

This early twentieth century photograph by Walter Harper of Broad Street shows the lawn and the surrounding rockery and garden belonging to the Bell House, situated on a terrace beside the River Teme. The net around the lawn suggests that it was sometimes used for tennis.

Cliff Villas, Ludford, c.1926. They were erected in 1841 by E.L. Charlton, the eccentric and litigious squire of Ludford, a man reputed to have fought the last duel in England. The gentleman on the cottage steps is believed to be William G. Kington, formerly a partner of Cliff & Kington, coachbuilders in Raven Lane, Ludlow.

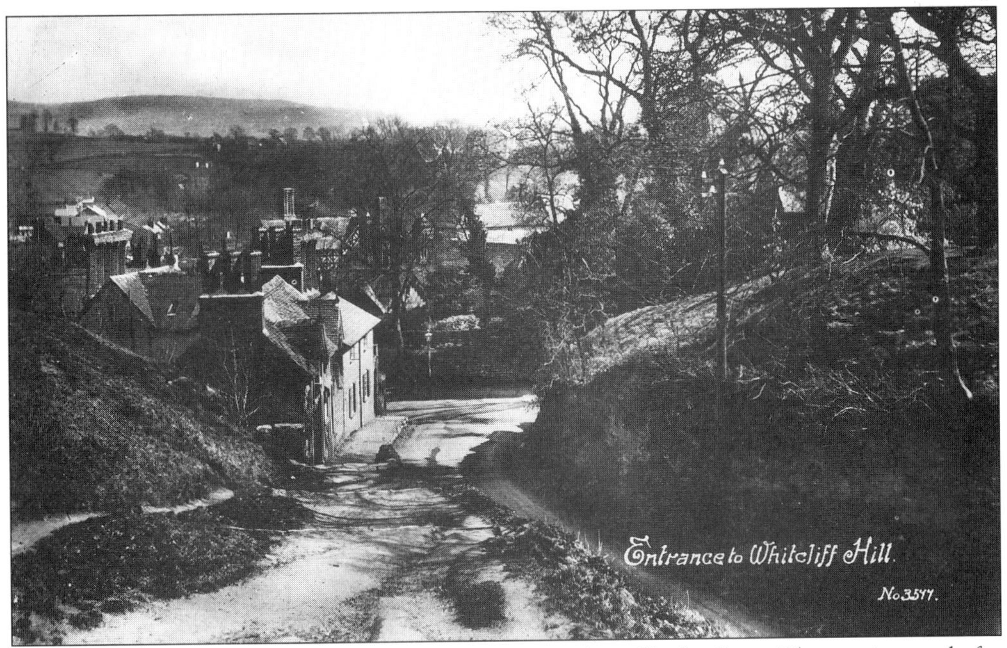

The road and steps descending from Whitcliffe towards Ludford village. The cutting made for the road provides a well known exposure of the Ludlow Bone Bed, much chiselled by geologists!

Almhouses at Ludford, as shown on a postcard published by J.C. Austen about 1906. In 1672 Sir Job Charlton of Ludford House, an eminent judge holding office at the Council of the Marches, endowed the almshouses with land and property. They were to accommodate "six poor and impotent persons", one of whom was to be Warden. These almshouses replaced a previous foundation by William Foxe of Ludford.

Seven

Later Suburbs

Until 1850 Ludlow was largely confined within its historic parish boundary though the pattern of roads, lanes and fields provided a framework for later growth. The earliest suburbs to develop were those along Gravel Hill and its subsidiary roads and around the small outlying settlement of East Hamlet. The first council estates - at Henley Road, Steventon, Temeside and Sandpits Avenue - were laid out in the 1920s and others were added after 1945. The post-Second World War period also saw a massive expansion of private housing,in a great crescent to the north, east and south-east of the town centre.

This part of Milton Road was built as a block of council flats in the late 1950s but was refurbished as a terrace of houses in the 1980s, just before this photograph was taken. The residents enjoy wide views across the town and beyond, with the tower of the parish church a prominent landmark.

A postcard view of Gravel Hill published soon after 1900 by E.E. Miller of 19 Corve Street. It shows an elegant late-Victorian suburb where a number of substantial houses were built. Several of these were for successful tradesmen who required more living space and larger gardens than were available in the town centre.

Gravel Hill, just outside St John's Church, 1955. The teenage rider is Eilleen Rhodes (now Warburton) and the child is Pat Mason who lived at the Limes, a large house just off the photograph to the left.

St Julian's Avenue, another residential area with large houses and spacious gardens, c.1900. The big house on the hill is Overmead, built before 1905 for Gaius Smith, the Ludlow grocer. The Croft, one of the houses on the right, was the home of Wilfred Dodgson, an estate agent who was a brother of Charles Dodgson, alias Lewis Carroll, the creator of *Alice in Wonderland*.

The lifestyle of one of Ludlow's leading commercial families is illustrated by this family snapshot taken at Hendra in 1929, then the home of Frederick Bodenham, draper and outfitter. His wife Alice is on the left and next to her, in a sun hat, is their daughter Muriel. Hendra House is now a residential home.

This terrace of houses and small shops was built at East Hamlet in the early 1880s by Benjamin and William Weale as part of their general development on the north side of New Road. East Hamlet School, opened in 1877, can be seen in the distance.

The largest and grandest building in East Hamlet is St Peter's Roman Catholic Church. Designed in a Byzantine style by an Italian architect, Rinvolucci, this building made a bold statement of faith when it was erected in the mid-1930s. It is now used by a large and devout congregation.

The Raven Inn in the 1930s with the landlord, Guss Smith, standing by the front door. The "Sign of the Raven" was transferred here from premises in Raven Lane in the 1860s, to cater to the thirst of a rapidly growing part of the town.

Two senior citizens take their ease at East Hamlet in the 1950s, on land later occupied by Helena Lane Home. In the distance one can see part of the Dodmore council estate, built to alleviate the acute housing shortage after the end of the Second World War.

Sandpits Avenue was the largest of Ludlow's pre-war council estates. Here the first four houses are being opened in 1929 by John Palmer, Mayor of Ludlow. The whole estate consists of blocks of four houses, each of which, at first, had their "privies" at the bottom of the garden.

Bill Hyde, a well-known resident of Sandpits Avenue seen here in the 1950s. Bill was a Midland Red driver who gave distinguished service to the Borough and Town councils for more that twenty-five years.

A 1949 photograph of Jean Forrester of 73 Sandpits Avenue (now Mrs Jean Morris of Lime Close). She was then a teenage employee of the Cosmo Dental Factory at the Case Mills in Temeside. The sweeping curve of "the Avenue" reflects the previous field pattern. There is still open countryside at the Sandpits Road end, soon to be developed as Riddings Road.

One of the outlying parts of Ludlow, beyond the modern bypass, is Rock's Green, like East Hamlet, an ancient township of Stanton Lacy parish. One of the public houses there was the New Inn, seen here in the early 1900s. The landlady, Mrs Susan Crowther, stands in front of the doorway surrounded by male customers. The property was later converted into a private home.

Eight
Earning a Living

The architectural delights and community facilities of Ludlow depend on its economic base. The town which we see and enjoy today has been created by the sweat and skill of our forebears; and continued economic viabilty is essential for Ludlow's future welfare. In the Middle Ages the burgesses produced much of their own food supply. They tended animals in enclosed meadows around the town and on Whitcliffe Common and cultivated crops in the large open fields which stretched from Prior's Halton in the west to Rock's Green in the east.

This detail from a painting of Ludlow Castle, made before 1772, shows haymaking in one of the meadows off Halton Lane. The artist was Paul Sandy, whose "clear, accurate and decorative manner" was "the archetype of British view painting".

A detail from a 1826 painting by Henry Zeigler showing a flock of sheep in Linney, with others grazing on the steep slopes below the castle. The shepherd chats to the woman and child, giving an unhurried air to the composition.

As late as 1974 cows could be seen crossing the A49 at the bottom of Corve Street. They were being moved from pasture in Linney to Stan Pipe's farm in St Mary's Lane, which leads off Corve Street just round the corner.

This detail from another of Ziegler's 1826 paintings shows tenter's racks in Lower Broad Street, behind the cloth manufactory of William Evans, the sole survivor of what had been Ludlow's leading industry until after 1600. The cloth was stretched and dried on these racks after fulling and dyeing.

This misericord from St Laurence's parish church gives a contemporary glimpse of Ludlow's medieval cloth trade. It shows a porter drawing on his boot and preparing for the road. The pack on his back is probably a bale of cloth, large numbers of which went from Ludlow to London, Bristol and parts of Europe.

Glovemaking later became Ludlow's leading industry. In the late eighteenth century the property shown on this 1978 photograph of Corve Street belonged to James Davies, one of the town's master glovers. The building on the right was the gloving workshop, with pivoting laths on the upper storey which could be opened to dry leather hung inside. The processed leather was cut on the premises and then sent for stitching into gloves by women and children working at home. The building was later used as a stable and has now been converted into a house.

A steam traction engine at Phoenix Ironworks, Gravel Hill, now occupied by Morris Bufton & Co. The proprietor, W.J. Roberts, who is standing in the left foreground, began the business in 1891. Variously described as iron and brass founders, agricultural engineers, and later as automobile engineers, the firm continued until the 1940s, at one time with more than forty employees.

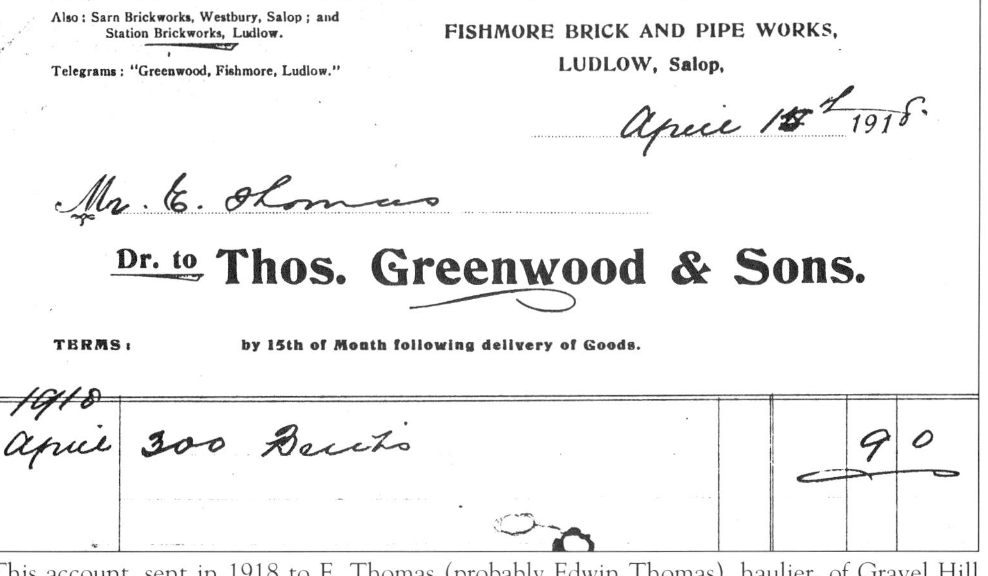

Also: Sarn Brickworks, Westbury, Salop; and Station Brickworks, Ludlow.

Telegrams: "Greenwood, Fishmore, Ludlow."

FISHMORE BRICK AND PIPE WORKS,
LUDLOW, Salop,

April 1st 1918.

Mr. E. Thomas

Dr. to **Thos. Greenwood & Sons.**

TERMS: by 15th of Month following delivery of Goods.

1918					
April	300 Bricks			9	0

This account, sent in 1918 to E. Thomas (probably Edwin Thomas), haulier, of Gravel Hill gives details of the last of the many firms that produced bricks in Ludlow from the late seventeenth century. Greenwood's premises were at the corner of Fishmore Road and New Road Bank. The works, which employed forty to fifty people, closed in 1940, though buildings and two tall chimneys remained until the 1950s. Part of the area is now occupied by Go Whittle coaches while the remainder, sadly, is derelict and overgrown.

The abnormal flood of June 1924 stimulated this photograph. It shows the River Corve in full spate and affords a distant view of the factory complex on Bromfield Road, still one of the largest industrial buildings in Ludlow. It was built to make parts for armaments in the First World War.

A group of workers on the Bromfield Road premises in 1956. They were employed by Veritas, who occupied part of the large building, manufacturing oil lamps, blow lamps and convector heaters. From left to right, back row: Harry Smith, Frances Stragwood (now Edwards), Jennifer Bennett (now Price), Ena Reynolds. Front row: Pat Sankey (now Ward), Bessie Morgan, Artie Collier, Doris Bennett.

This picture taken from the church tower in 1978 shows Ludlow's two largest post-Second World War industrial enterprises. In the foreground, behind the Clifton Cinema and other Old Street buildings, are the worksheds of E.W. Walters & Co. (Ludlow) Ltd, clothing manufacturers, occupying what was once called Sutton's Close. Beyond can be seen the Temeside Works of F.W. McConnel Ltd, engineers, who make and export a wide range of agricultural machinery.

The interior of part of Walters' factory photographed by Peter Bartlett in the 1980s. The firm, which makes trousers and other garments, began in the redundant Methodist church in Old Street in 1958 with just five employees. It became Ludlow's largest employer with branches in several other places.

Manual workers with their spades and picks were an important part of any town economy. Here men installing an electricity cable at Gravel Hill in 1905 rest on their tools as they and their supervisors pose for a photograph.

The workforce which completed the laboratories and other new buildings at Ludlow Grammar School in 1928.

Ludlow's primary function through eight centuries has been as a market centre. Central to this is the livestock market, held until the nineteenth century in the historic High Street, but then moved to the edge of town. This is a view of the livestock market in Corve Street in 1916, when the auctioneers were Davies and Edwards. The rails between the stalls were then made of wood.

Some marketing went on in other parts of Ludlow, such as this sale of Christmas poultry, an annual event at the Bell Inn in Upper Galdeford. The vendors are posing for a photograph before the customers are admitted.

Retailing is another form of marketing and early records of the town abound with "selda" or stalls. This detail of a drawing made in 1846 shows the open shop front of what is now the Comus bar of the Feathers at No. 25 Bull Ring. The premises were then occupied by a butcher, William Ward Evans. He can be seen chopping meat in the left hand window, while customers wait on the right. The lady in the first floor room is perhaps Mrs Evans.

The shop of Peachey Brothers, fishmongers and gamemongers, at No. 7 Tower Street, taken just before the First World War. The business was later moved to larger premises in Corve Street.

The premises of Freeman, Hardy & Willis, at No. 42 Bull Ring, on the corner with Tower Street. The staff pose for a set photograph. This national multiple firm of boot and shoe dealers had traded in Broad Street from the early years of the twentieth century, but moved to the Bull Ring in the 1920s. They are still in business in Ludlow, now at Nos. 9/10 King Street.

An early picture of the shop front of A.J. Roberts, a local businessman who opened at No. 55 Broad Street in 1927, later occupying the adjoining premises at No. 56. Goods on display included dollies for washing, dolly tubs (note the protruding ledges for soap) and builders' sieves. The row of watering cans right of the steps were made to what was called "the Ludlow pattern".

There were a number of small shops in the residential parts of Ludlow, as there still are in some places. One of these was the grocery business on Sandpits Road, facing Sandpits Avenue, which was run from 1933 until 1971 by Mr & Mrs J.L. Briggs.

The interior of the Sandpits Road shop, with the owners reviewing their goods. They gave excellent and friendly service and it was always known as a happy shop.

Photographs of shop interiors are rare, but this image, unfortunately sadly deteriorated, shows the inside of the London Tea Company in the early 1920s, crowded with china and a range of other goods. The manager, on the far right, is Mr John Detheridge.

The interior of No. 60 Broad Street in the 1890s, when it was occupied by Edward Robinson, watchmaker and jeweller. The business was continued by his son, Geoffrey, until after the Second World War. Geoffrey Robinson married Florence Pugh, a local suffragette who later became a J.P. and a long serving member of the Red Cross.

Coaches for affluent passengers and mail became more frequent during the eighteenth century, as roads were turnpiked and improved. One of the principal coaching inns was the Angel in Broad Street, shown on this tradecard of Benjamin Fieldhouse, who was landlord there in the 1790s.

Large waggons pulled by teams of horses were used to transport parcels, commercial goods and poorer passengers. This 1801 painting of *The Parcel Post of Ludlow* is by a Swiss artist, Jaques-Laurent Agasse (1767-1849). The location is unknown but the waggon is probably that of Robert Taylor, which took five and a half days to travel between his warehouse in Corve Street, Ludlow and the George Inn, Smithfield, in London.

The railway from Shrewsbury to Ludlow was opened on 20 April 1852 and was extended to Hereford in 1853. The earliest known picture of any part of Ludlow station is this engraving by the Ludlow artist, William Gwynn (1782-1860). The building on the left is the engine shed.

Ludlow station looking south, showing the "up" platform and the main station buildings, 1967. This photograph was taken by Charles Underhill, a local railway enthusiast, just before the buildings were demolished.

One of the first two commercial garages in the town was the Ludlow Motor Garage, which by 1909 was established at No. 140 Corve Street. This later expanded up the hill to absorb No. 141 and by the 1920s had become the Ludlow Motor Company.

The staff of Castle Garage in the early 1950s, seated outside their original premises at the top of Mill Street. Jack Price, founder of the firm, is third from the left in the front row. The garage later moved to a more spacious site in Corve Street.

Nine
Government

Though Ludlow was not incorporated as a parliamentary borough until 1461, a tradition of almost complete self government by 12 Aldermen and 25 Common Councillors goes back much further. This became a self-electing oligarchic Corporation, drawing some members from land-owning families around the town, and headed by a High Bailiff and a Low Bailiff who held office for one year. In 1835 the Corporation was replaced by an elected Borough Council of 4 Aldermen and 12 Councillors, one of whom served as Mayor.

From 1889 the newly constituted Shropshire County Council accepted increasing responsibility for major services in all Shropshire towns. Since then Ludlow has had one elected member on the County Council. In 1967, as part of a national reorganisation of local government, many of the remaining responsibilities of the Borough Council passed to Ludlow Rural District Council, which became South Shropshire District Council in 1974. At present 9 of the 40 elected members represent Ludlow. A Town Council of 15 elected members, one of whom serves as Mayor, still provides a number of local services and employs a staff headed by the Town Clerk. Ceremonies include an annual Mayor Making each May, which incorporates some of the features of the ancient ritual of Bailiffs' Change, a major event in the social calendar of pre-Reform Ludlow.

A tree planting ceremony in 1905, to commemorate the coming of age of Viscount Windsor Clive of Oakly Park, a family which had maintained a close and largely benevolent interest in the Borough of Ludlow since the eighteenth century. The Mayor, wearing his chain of office, was Henry Lloyd, a Corve Street maltster. On the right are John Williams, Town Clerk, and John Flattery, Common Sergeant.

A sizeable crowd is shown supporting the Mayor, Councillor Richard Poyner, and Borough Council at the opening of Coronation Avenue on 20 February 1931. The ceremony was performed by Sir Henry Maybury, who is next but one to the left of the Mayor. He was Director General of the Roads Department at the Ministry of Transport from 1919. He worked for a firm of contractors in Ludlow in the early 1890s and married a Ludlow girl, Elizabeth Sheldon.

A less formal occasion in 1964, taking place in the Bull Ring, outside the premises of W.H. Smith. The Countess of Plymouth was inaugurating a scheme for street improvement, supported by the Mayor, Councillor Gladys Potter and her daughter Celia (now Celia Rowlands, J.P.) who was Mayoress. Those standing include Police Superindent Jones and, to the left, Muriel Curry (née Bodenham).

The Borough Council leaving St Laurence's parish church by the west door on 14 July 1951 after a service to mark the Festival of Britain. The Mayor, a tall and elegant figure, was Harry Little, an inland revenue official. Behind him can be seen Alderman Richard Poyner and Alderman Violet Packer. The Common Sergeant, carrying the large mace, was John Evans of Old Street, and the Mace Bearer, carrying the two small maces, was Bill Jeffs. Bill later became Common Sergeant and filled the office with pride and dignity until 1991.

The Borough Council, in spite of fierce debates and differences of opinion, enjoyed great local prestige, and service on it was considered a considerable honour. Several of the councillors shown above, including Gladys Potter, Violet Packer, Ted Sheldon and Bill Price, were active promoters of the town's first swimming baths in Dinham, which opened in 1959. Much of the money was raised through weekly subscriptions to the Ludlow Guild. The picture shows Ludlow Borough Council and employees in 1954.

From left to right, back row: T. Fewtrell, office; M. Paragreen, office; H. Morris, office; W. Jones, Town Clerk's secretary; R. Thatcher, rent clerk; B. Nicholls, office; E. Scivell, office; A.Evans, office. Second row: W. Jeffs, Common Sergeant; Cllr R. Ashton; Cllr G. Bellwood; Cllr E. Sheldon; Cllr R. Wakeman; Cllr H. Little; Cllr J. Davies; Cllr G.E. Judd; Cllr C. Grimmett; Cllr G. Potter; Cllr W. Price; W. Allum, Mace Bearer. Front row: J. James, Borough Surveyor; Alderman H. Keyse; Alderman A. Gatehouse; Alderman V. Packer; Bishop E.W. Sara, Mayor's Chaplain; Cllr S. Price, Mayor; R. Price, Mayoress; J. Mallony, Town Clerk; Mrs Price, wife of the Mayor; Alderman T.B. Yarrow; J. Wisdom, Borough Treasurer.

Opposite: Ludlow Borough Council inherited the right to bestow the title of Honourary Burgess. In the twentieth century this has been used sparingly as a recognition of exceptional public service. Here three honorary burgesses, Doctor James Egan, Alderman Gladys Potter and Alderman Violet Packer are seen in 1967 with one of only two surviving hereditary burgesses, the Earl of Plymouth, whose family inherited the Oakly Park estates of the Clives.

One link between the pre-1835 Borough Corporation and the Town Council of the 1990s is the Town Plate. It is seen here on display in the Town Hall at the annual Mayor Making ceremony, guarded by the macebearers. On the right is Norman Price, Mace Bearer from 1955 to 1992.

The offices of South Shropshire District Council are located in and around Stone House in Corve Street, a large house built about 1840 by descendants of the Actons, one of Ludlow's most prosperous glove manufacturing families.

A meeting in February 1992 of the Economic Development and Leisure Committee, one of four standing committees of the District Council. The chairman, in the centre of the platform, was Ken Habershon, councillor for Lydbury North since 1973. He is flanked by senior officers including, from the left: James Caird, Director of Planning; Maurice Bullen, Director of Finance; Graham Biggs, Chief Executive; and Bill Jones, Director of Operational Services.

National politics have had a turbulent history in Ludlow, especially at the notorious election of 1839, when there was "gross corruption and treating" on both sides, with "bludgeon men" brought in from outside. Here a large crowd at the Butter Cross awaits the result of the February 1910 election. This was the time when the reforming Liberal government appealed for national backing in its bid to limit the power of the House of Lords. The Liberals won nationally but in Ludlow and South Shropshire the Conservative candidate, Rowland Hunt, had a majority of 2,404.

Jo Grimond, leader of the Liberal party, visited Ludlow in 1964. With him is the chairman of the local party, Fred Reeves. An outstanding teacher of history at Ludlow Grammar School from 1928 to 1965, Fred Reeves was prominent in a range of local affairs, and was Chairman of the Civic Society for many years.

Many members of the royal family were associated with Ludlow's early history. Visits this century have been less frequent but invariably attract great public interest. The Princess of Wales, later Queen Mary, visited Ludlow on 24 November 1909. Here she is walking along Castle Street (left picture) accompanied by the Mayor, George Woodhouse, the Bull Ring chemist. The Princess later attended service at St Laurence's parish church. She is seen here (right picture) leaving through the west door. An escort was provided by the Ludlow Boys Brigade.

Borough councillors and their wives are presented to H.R.H. Princess Margaret, before the 1959 performance of *Comus* at Ludlow Castle. This marked the successful completion of a seven year campaign to raise funds for the restoration of the wooden roof and stonework of St Laurence's parish church. The lady curtseying is Mrs Keyse, while Alderman Keyse looks on. To the right are Cllr Jack Davies, who had just completed two years as Mayor, and Mrs Ida Davies, who still lives in Ludlow.

Ten

Body, Mind and Soul

Like other towns, Ludlow has a range of institutions, some of them venerable and long established, which provide for the spiritual, bodily and intellectual needs of its citizens. Most enduring of these is the parish church, the tower of which was used by the Worcestershire poet and classical scholar, A.E. Housman, as an image of stability in a world of change and sorrow:

Leave your home behind, lad,
And reach your friends your hand,
And go, and luck go with you,
While Ludlow tower shall stand

Housman's ashes are buried in Ludlow churchyard and the centenary of his most famous publication, *A Shropshire Lad*, will be celebrated in 1996.

The clergy in 1889. Seated in the centre is Rev Ffaringdon Clayton, a formidable personality who was rector from 1867 to 1907. In 1874 he had married Victoria Clive, the youngest sister of George Windsor Clive, Ludlow's M.P. from 1860 until the end of Borough representation in 1885.

Prebendary John Baulch, Rector of Ludlow (1984-1993), greets Vic Roberts, who became team vicar in the Ludlow Six Parishes established during these years. The community was stunned when John, a London Eastender with a great sense of purpose and rare social gifts, died of cancer whilst still incumbent.

The church choir in the 1950s. In the centre is Bishop E.W. Sara, rector from 1945 to 1963. To the right is Ellis Shaw, later to become Chairman of the Friends of St Laurence. Three places left of the rector is Harold Burton, formerly Head of Ludlow Senior School. On the far right is Jack Potts, a dedicated verger for many years.

Senior members of the Parochial Church Council in the early 1960s. From left to right: H.J. Turpin, customs and excise officer; S.R. Burgess, auctioneer; J.R. Richardson, banker; F. Tipton, Ludlow post office; W. Summers, Head of Ludlow Secondary Modern School. Mr Turpin's elder son, Kenneth, became Warden of Oriel College, Oxford, and Vice-Chancellor of the University.

This building, now used as a scout hut and for other social purposes, was erected as a Roman Catholic church in Julian Road in 1906. There had been a small number of Roman Catholic families in Ludlow since the sixteenth century, while a number of local landowners including the Blounts of Mawley Hall and the Plowdens of Plowden were of that faith.

The interior of the building as it was when used as a church. The priest here for many years was Father Charles Fisher, while Armel and Violet O'Connor of Mary's Meadow in Steventon were regular members of the congregation. The latter's *Mary's Meadow Papers*, published in 1915, is a moving testimony to her faith.

Non-conformists were for many years a minority in Ludlow, but their churches thrived in the first half of the nineteenth century, and in 1861 it was reported that half the town's population were non-conformist. The picture shows the interior of the town's first Congregational Church, built in a yard off the lower part of Corve Street in the 1730s. This early photograph, taken from the sanctuary, shows the church lavishly decorated for harvest festival. The church was demolished in the 1960s.

The pulpit and some pews inside the new Congregational Church which was built off Old Street in 1830. The church closed in the 1960s through lack of members and was converted into a private house by Paul and Betty Smith. Paul Smith, now retired, was one of the most highly regarded of Ludlow's many post-Second World War antique dealers.

Although Charles Wesley married Sarah Gwynn, whose family had a town house in Ludlow, Methodism was late to develop in the town. There were three flourishing churches in the nineteenth century, one of which, the Wesleyan Church in Broad Street, is represented here by its choir, photographed inside St Mary's Chapel in the castle. Standing on the stone ledge at the back: W.H. Cliff, coach builder and organist; Mr Toft; H. Amphlett, photographer.
From left to right, standing at back: Rev H. Needham, junior minister; Miss Tomlinson; Miss Sanders; Mr J. Barker, Headmaster of the British School; Mr F. Blackbourne, choirmaster; Mr R.A. Wynne; Rev E. Ashton Jones, supervising minister; Mr E. Cookson; Mr T. Micklewright, cabinet maker; Mr R.E. Crundall, newsagent.
Sitting: Mrs W.H. Cliff; Miss A. Micklewright; Miss Harding; Mr W. Harding, former choirmaster and retired school attendance officer; Miss F. Vale; Mrs Larcombe; Miss F. Micklewright.
Kneeling: Miss L. Davies; Miss F. Davies; Miss B. Packer; Miss M. Crundall.

Another nonconformist choir, that of the Primitive Methodist Church in 1873, the year that their new church opened in Old Street (now part of the premises of E. Walters Ltd (Ludlow). The church was built by William Russell who is standing at the left of the back row. The photograph was taken in the garden of the Preacher's House, where Russell lived.

The Baptist Church in Rock Lane, which was built in 1868, with the schoolroom added in 1877. This picture shows the congregation in September 1994, when a service was held here prior to moving to new premises at the Rockspring Centre, which combines a church with community facilities.

The oldest endowed institution in Ludlow is Hosier's Almshouses, founded in 1463 by John Hosier, a rich cloth merchant. The Borough Corporation became Trustees and commissioned the present building in 1758, with the town arms proudly displayed on the pediment.

This timber-framed house in Old Street, now a private residence, was acquired for use as a workhouse and house of correction in the late seventeenth century, using money bequeathed by Thomas Lane, secretary to Sir Job Charlton of Ludford.

In 1838 the Board of Guardians for Ludlow and the surrounding district opened a new workhouse at Gravel Hill with accommodation for up to three hundred paupers. When this photograph was taken, in the 1950s, it had become a hospital in the National Health Service. It was later much improved and extended to fulfill its present role as East Hamlet Hospital.

The governors and staff of Ludlow Cottage Hospital in June 1948, when it became part of the National Health Service. Some of those in the photograph still live in Ludlow, including its donor, Sister Chinn, now Mrs Hayes of No. 41 Mill Street. From left to right, back row: B.N. Fletcher (Hon. Secretary), H.J. Dennis, Mrs Cook, Miss Hughes, Miss Berkeley, Mrs Bennett, Miss Davies, Miss M.S. Haylock. Centre: I.A. Slater, C.T. Marston, Dr Fenton, Nurses Martin, Dodd, Morgan, Boulton and Shuker, H.J. Clee, Dr Hooker, Dr Roberts. Front row: Nurses MacDonald, Yemm and Taylor, Sister Chinn, Miss Clayton (Trustee), Bishop Sara (Chairman), Miss M.A. Clifford (Matron), Miss Venables, Sisters James and Jones.

There was a church grammar school in Ludlow as early as 1200. Later, the school was operated by the Palmers Guild, then by the Borough Corporation and from 1876 by its own board of governors. In 1977 the school became Ludlow Sixth Form College, which still benefits from the ancient endowment. This picture of the school dates from before 1802. A stone house built about 1390 was acquired in 1527, its solar wing becoming the Headmaster's house visible on the far left. The dormer windows were inserted in 1686 to light roof dormitories for boarders.

The school on Speech Day, July 1914. The portly clergyman is an Old Ludlovian, Canon E.F. Smith, Vicar of Tewkesbury, who distributed the prizes. To the right is the Headmaster, R.B. Threlfall, and beyond him three masters who remained on the staff until 1945 or later: H.S. Breakspear, science, and Headmaster from 1936; W.H. Sparshatt, Latin; and C.M. Davenport King, commercial subjects and school bursar.

The schoolroom in 1956, after some of the roof timbers exposed in 1909 had been restored. This historic room is now Ludlow College Library. The school at this time enjoyed a high academic reputation, sending a steady stream of boys to Oxbridge and other universities. Between 1951 and 1964 more than 40 boys gained Oxbridge places, seven of them with open awards! Extra-curricular activities thrived, with school plays being taken on tour in Europe while in 1955 Clive Lewis, the school rugby captain, played twice for England Schoolboys, scoring a memorable try against Wales.

In 1855 the Church of England's National Society erected a new school building in Lower Galdeford for the children of the poor. The central hall was for infants and the wings for boys and girls. The building later accommodated Ludlow Senior School and then Ludlow Secondary Modern School. Much altered and extended, this is now the Bishop Mascall Centre, an educational and training centre for Hereford diocese.

A class at Ludlow Senior School in the 1920s, under the watchful eye of the Headmaster, John Diggle. The boy on the right in the front row, Thomas Collins, became supervisor of the Roads and Bridges Division of Shropshire County Council.

The five headmistresses of the Ludlow National and Infants Schools in the early 1900s. New schools were opened at East Hamlet in the 1870s, to supplement those at Galdeford. Miss Elizabeth Cantrell, seated on the left, was Head of the Galdeford Infants School for 45 years, from January 1868 to December 1912.

Ludlow Girls' High School opened in 1910, using as its main building an elegant Georgian house in Castle Square. The large window on the second floor was created for the school's first laboratory. It aimed to provide secondary education for girls comparable to that available to boys at the Grammar School.

The school hall, added in 1938, is here being used in the early 1960s for physical education.

A school for the children of non-conformists, which started in 1870, was established in Old Street as the British School in 1898. This group of children in the early 1930s includes Harry Peachey, a well known Ludlow business man and personality (front row, third from right), and Phyllis (P.D.) James, now Baroness James the novelist, at the far left of the fourth row back.

Before the High School opened, there were many private girls' academies and seminaries in Ludlow. This is an 1871 group from Mrs Watson's School, based at Castle Lodge, but seen here on a visit to the castle.

A tradition of enterprise and high achievement in extra-curricular activities in Ludlow schools has been continued in recent years. Here Ludlow School performers take a curtain call at the Albert Hall in 1987 after their performance of *Prometheus* at the finals of a national competition sponsored by Barclays Bank. The school won first prize and was highly praised for its performance.

One of the scenes from the production, which was directed by Tony Knight, a senior member of staff. The themes were explored through music, mime and dance. The girl in the centre is Alice Hooton.

Eleven
Recreation

Ludlow has a long tradition of popular sports and pastimes. One of these was the annual tug of war on Shrove Tuesday, when people from Castle and Broad Street wards pulled against those from Old Street and Corve Street wards. This was discontinued in the 1850s after at least one fatality had occurred.

There was a fair in Ludlow in the twelfth and thirteenth centuries on 1 May, the festival of St Philip and St James, to whom the parish church was then dedicated. Later this was discontinued but it was restarted in the 1820s, primarily for the sale of livestock and the hiring of servants, though many traditional May day festivities soon became attached to the event. The latter encouraged the survival of the occasion after other annual fairs gave way to fortnightly or weekly livestock markets. An annual pleasure fair is still held for four days in the town centre around or close to 1 May and is attended by people from all sections of the community, both from Ludlow itself and from the surrounding countryside.

The lads in their hundreds to Ludlow come in for the fair,
There's men from the barn and the forge and the mill and the fold,
The lads for the girls and the lads for the liquor are there,
And there with the rest are the lads that will never be old.

A.E. Housman, A Shropshire Lad *(1896)*

Part of the fair in what was then called Post Office Square, early 1900s. On the right is a large steam roundabout.

Maypole dancing was well established in Ludlow and in the nineteenth century it took place in Galdeford, Dinham and Holdgate Fee. A maypole was standing in the latter as late as 1876. Here children revive the custom as part of the 1934 Shropshire Pageant.

Folk dancing of many kinds was popular, a nineteenth century report referring to "as many as twenty fiddlers and dancing couples reaching the whole length of the street". Morris and folk dancing were revived in Ludlow in the early 1950s, as seen here in Castle Square in 1951, during the Festival of Britain celebrations. Arthur Reynolds, a furniture manufacturer, and his family were the chief promoters of this activity.

Other kinds of dancing were led by Fury's Dance Band, here seen at the back of the Town Hall in the 1930s. From left to right the players were Ted Fury, Brian Fury, Jack Fury and Pat Fury, with Arthur Powis, a well known local musician, helping out on the right.

The Young Conservatives Ball in the 1930s, held in the functions room behind No. 22 Broad Street. Sitting on the left of the drum are Mrs Windsor Clive, Colonel Windsor Clive, who was Conservative M.P. for South Shropshire, and Miss John, hostess for the evening.

There has been horse racing on the Old Field at Bromfield since the 1720s or earlier. The annual race meeting, usually held in July, was a highspot in Ludlow's social calendar, as in 1777, when five lords attended. This picture shows the opening of the New Stand in 1907.

Ludlow had a rare day of glory in 1932 when a local horse, Forbra, won the Grand National. Here the horse is shown with the owner, William Parsonage, in front of his home at Sunnymead in Burway Lane. The trainer, T. Rimmell, is on the right. William Parsonage, who was Mayor of Ludlow that year, celebrated the occasion by giving every schoolchild one penny!

Pigeon racing – "the fancy" – has long been very popular in Ludlow. Here a Ludlow baker, Gerald Price, is pictured in front of the pigeon lofts at the bottom of his garden in Bromfield Road. The care and training of pigeons is taken very seriously in the town, as in 1990, when the Town Council agreed to resite a lamp standard in Rock Lane because the light was disturbing neighbouring pigeons.

A slightly younger Gerald Price and two fellow enthusiasts, Jack Angel (centre) and Mike Tipton, with prize-winning pigeons and certificates.

A football club was in existence at Ludlow by 1876 or earlier. Here the 1907-08 team and members of the club are seen at Sandpits Road.

This poster was found in a time capsule buried beneath the Town Hall in 1888 and recovered when the building was demolished in March 1986. Wolverhampton Wanderers were then emerging as a leading professional club but research has shown that the team playing Ludlow Town was in fact the Reserves. No record of the result has yet been found!

Ludlow and South Shropshire Cricket Club was first recorded in 1848. It played its first matches at Ludford Park but later shared a large and very lovely ground at Burway with Ludlow Grammar School, leased from Plymouth Estates. This postcard shows a match on the Grammar School part of the ground in the 1930s.

The Ludlow and South Shropshire First Eleven cricket team, 1921. From left to right, back row: L.T. Vine Stevens (umpire), W. Parsonage, -?-, G.E.D. Shorting, O. Gibbon, H.O.H. Wenman, T. Cooper. Front row: C.M. Davenport King, S.W. Marston, P.H. Ludlow (Captain), T.C. Green, J.W. Clarke, L.W. Parsonage (scorer).

The Burway Bowling Club was formed in 1909, as an offshoot of Ludlow and South Shropshire Cricket Club. The pavilion was bought for £20 from the Polo Club at Bromfield! The picture shows club members in the 1950s. From left to right, back row: Heber Reynolds, William Mapp, Tom Brindley, Bill Shelley, -?-, Fred Faulkner, John Evans, -?-, E. Lewis. Third row: Hughie Badlan, -?-, -?-, Stan Davies, -?-, Charlie Judd, Wilfred Parsonage, -?-, Wilfred Packer, Alf Lewis, Tom Lloyd, E.S. Hennen. Second row: Tom Davies, Bill Price, Stan Stephens, Val Cheadle, Harry Little, Harry Keyse, Dick Howard, Hughie Lockhart, J. Wyness. Front row: -?-, W.H. Latham, Jack Parsonage, Bill Atack, Harry Jones, -?-, Jimmy James, Dennis Watkins.

Four members of the Burway Bowling Club on the green.

This photograph by Jane Green, taken about 1900, shows a group of young ladies and gentlemen, mounted on bicycles, in some kind of tournament taking place in Linney, on land which later became the Castle Sports Club.

Members of the Castle Tennis Club at Linney in the early 1930s. Those identified are from left to right, back row: Edwin Faraday, -?-, Jack Sanderson, -?-, Bill Cartwright. Front row: Doris Price, Flo Trune, -?-, Jessie Jones, -?-, -?-, Tommy Wainwright.

When they were opened in 1840, the Assembly Rooms, with a spacious ballroom on the first floor, became the town's principal venue for dances, concerts and other social gatherings. As leisure patterns changed, these buildings were later used for a variety of purposes, and one of the earliest small picture houses in the country opened here in 1909. Initially, this was called "The Picture Hall" and was operated by Alfred Temple, a travelling showman, who bought the whole block in 1920.

The Clifton Cinema, a fine example of inter-war architecture, opened in Old Street in 1938, replacing some of the town's worst slums at Noakes' Yard and Dean's Yard. In the mid-1970s, as the decline in cinema-going nationally reached crisis proportions, it was used as a Bingo Hall. In 1986, after a contentious planning decision, the building was demolished.

LUDLOW NATURAL HISTORY SOCIETY.

THE MUSEUM.

Splendid collections of the following :-

British & Foreign Birds.
Birds eggs & nests.
Silurian Fossils.
Minerals.
Recent shells.
Geological models.

Relics from Ludlow Castle and Neighbourhood.
Pre-historic remains.
Ancient Weapons.
Documents and many other Objects of interest.

J. Palmer & W.C.D la Touche Hon: Secs.

Mr Steele — Caretaker.

Admission sixpence

This poster from c.1910 catches the ethos of what was still essentially a Victorian museum. The geological collections here, assembled by Sir Roderick Murchison and local collaborators in the 1830s, were of great scientific importance.

Gardening and the enjoyment of gardens have been recreations in Ludlow for several centuries. This Edwardian postcard shows the lower part of the garden behind No. 14 Castle Street, then the home of Miss M.E. Green and family. The trees on the right overlook the town wall while towers of the domestic range at the castle provide a dramatic background. The garden is now part of a public carpark!

The pleasures of relaxation can be enjoyed in small gardens as well as large. Here Trevor Davies, a railway employee, and Jack Lloyd, his brother-in-law, recline in deck chairs amidst the garden flowers of one of the council houses between Sandpits Road and Henley Road.

A different kind of relaxation can be had in the town's public houses. One such inn is the Blue Boar in Mill Street, photographed here early in the twentieth century. The landlord, Harold Burmingham, stands in shirt sleeves outside the front door, with four of his customers. His grandson, Don Burmingham of Housman Crescent, and great-grandson, Vince Burmingham of Keystone Gardens, are well-known Ludlow citizens today.

Regulars and passers-by pose outside the Globe in Market Street, 1880s. The flags suggest that the occasion may have been Queen Victoria's Golden Jubilee in 1887. Public houses continue to play a prominent role in Ludlow's leisure patterns, darts, dominoes and quizzes all being popular in the 1990s.

Uniformed youth organisations flourished in Ludlow in the twentieth century. Here, in 1910, the First Ludlow Boy Scouts are grouped in Castle Gardens, near their headquarters in Dinham. The scoutmaster, moustached and right of centre, was Joseph Bessell, a High Street tailor.

The Ludlow Brownies in the outer bailey of the castle in 1927. From left to right, back row: Mary Stewardson, -?-, Nancy French, Una Ratty, -?-, Gertie Mapp, Winnie Jones, Lucy Davies, Betty Wainwright, -?-, Dorothy Gore. Middle row: Jewel Cash, Muriel Nutt, Nancy Gore, Melba Booth, Emily Heapy, Mary Beddoes, Amy Wainwright, Eileen Watson, Kath Pinches, Mary Nutt, Mary Harding. Front row: -?-, Freda Thomas, Millie Paragreen, Vera Ratty, Miss Evans, Mrs Lovat, Betty Beddoes, -?-, Rita Kenhard.

The Ludlow Junior Imperial League Dance, held in the Town Hall in the early 1920s. Patriotic feeling ran strong in the town at this time and Empire Day was an important event. The picture is a reminder of the many enjoyable social occasions held at the Town Hall.

Many social activities revolved round the churches. This is a day out for the "Happy Gathering" group of the Gospel Hall Church, who met in the former Primitive Methodist Church in Old Street. The church had members from all social groups, but was justly proud of the help it gave in poorer parts of the town.

Carnivals have been popular in Ludlow from time to time. This float parked outside the gas show rooms in Broad Street was an entry for one of the trade carnivals in the 1930s, organised by Ludlow Chamber of Commerce. The man by the horse's head is Ben Williams; he is still resident in Ludlow.

There is a tradition of street parties in some parts of Ludlow. This shows participants at such an event in Sandpits Avenue in 1953, celebrating the Coronation. In the centre is Herbert Bufton, grandfather of the present editor of *The Ludlow Advertiser*. Herbert had been Regimental Sergeant Major with the King's Shropshire Light Infantry in the First World War, and was decorated three times. He is flanked by other members of the Bufton family, while in front are the children of Joe Beniams, a Midland Red driver.

Twelve
Wartime

The early history of Ludlow is crowded with military events, but there have been no hostilities since the summer of 1646, when Parliamentary troops besieged and eventually captured the town. However, regiments have often been quartered here or in the neighbouring countryside and in 1689 the Royal Welch Fusiliers were first mustered and trained in the castle, before marching to their first engagement at the Battle of the Boyne. Many Ludlow men have served with distinction in the armed forces, right up to the present day, one of the most notable being "old Davies", who was buried in December 1750, reputedly aged 112. He had ridden with the light horse when the Duke of Monmouth was defeated at Sedgemoor in 1685.

Both the World Wars made a great impact on the lives of Ludlow people. Many men and women served overseas, large numbers of troops were stationed in or near the town, and local organisations were formed to provide support services. The town escaped direct enemy action, except for one unexploded bomb which fell near College Street in 1941, but convoys of military vehicles regularly passed through, and in the Second World War there were floods of evacuees.

Postcards such as this were issued for many towns in the First World War, helping to boost the patriotic fervour which swept the country in 1914.

These First World War soldiers, photographed by local photographer, C.E. Amphlett, were probably camping just outside Ludlow, perhaps at Ludford Park, which is known to have been used for military purposes.

Soldiers of the Royal Army Medical Corps marching out of Ludlow on 10 May 1915.

Nurses of the Red Cross lined up in good military order close to Portcullis Lane during the First World War. The picture provides a rare glimpse of Portcullis Lane, the ancient parish boundary between Ludlow (beyond) and Stanton Lacy (foreground). On the left can be seen No. 12 Portcullis Lane, a small house later demolished to provide the present car park.

Convalescent soldiers outside Overmead, the large house in Livesey Road, which became a nursing home during the First World War. One of the nurses here was Florence Pugh (later Robinson), a well known Ludlow citizen who remained active in the Red Cross for many years; she also served as a magistrate.

Two Ludlow "tommies" were John (right) and Arthur French of Lower Broad Street, seen here together in Belgium in September 1944. Three days later, Arthur, a Corporal in the King's Shropshire Light Infantry, showed "courageous and determined leadership" in destroying two German anti-tank gun batteries with a section of six men, for which he was later awarded the Military Medal. John was killed in Holland later in the month.

The first Ludlovian to die in action in World War Two was a former Grammar School boy, Pilot Officer Laurie Whitbread, who was shot down over north Kent on 15 September 1940, the day generally accepted as a turning point in the Battle of Britain. Serving under Group Captain Douglas Bader, Laurie had shot down or damaged a number of German planes earlier in the battle. He is pictured here with one of the Spitfires in which he sometimes flew.

Platoon "F" (Ludlow) Company of the Home Guard, recruited rapidly in the summer of 1940 and photographed here in February 1942. Captain A.W. Churchill, who lived at "Hylands", Bromfield, is in the middle of the front row. To the left is Captain Charles Lloyd, a local dentist. The platoon took part in a number of training exercises, including a mock battle at Dinham Bridge in May 1943, which local people were invited to watch from the castle walks.

The Ludlow first aid post in the outer bailey of the castle in December 1941. From left to right, back row: W. Griffin, G.W. Scriven, J.T. Wiles, C.J. Detheridge, E.C. Kirby, T.K. Corbishly, V.J. Cheadle, A. Scriven. Middle row: W.J. Morris, C.J. Price, R. Page, J.A. Sanderson, E.O. Phillips, T.J. Fewtrell, J.G. Davies, R. Bebbington, W.E. Price, W. Jaine. Front row: L.A. Richards, F.G. Lang, J.W. Jackson, Dr E.C. Abraham, J.P. Preece, W.J. Munns, S.R. Hayes.

This picture, enlarged from a snapshot taken by Pat Snow (now Perry) shows soldiers on Ludford Bridge, one of whom, on the right, appears to be a prisoner of war, probably from the large camp at the Sheet. The traffic sign is a reminder of the many convoys which came through the town during the war years.

This photograph, probably taken on Sunday or in the evening during the early 1940s, shows soldiers and civilians walking in High Street. The sign of Mrs Beeston's cafe is just visible, to the right of the parked car.

Part of the queue waiting for entry to the Picture House early in the Second World War. Servicemen and their girlfriends are prominent. Most of the RAF were no doubt from the large camp at Ludford, later occupied by Americans. The Castle Lodge Annexe Cafe, run by Percy Brown, was a popular rendezvous at that time.

During the war years women had to undertake many of the jobs usually done by men. Here the Mayor, Alderman Brown, congratulates Mary Howard (now Williams) who operated a daily street cleaning service in the 1940s with her horse and cart.

A detachment of the Ludlow branch of the British Legion follows the band at the head of a Remembrance Day parade in the 1960s. Based at Victory House at No. 8 Mill Street, the Legion has been active in keeping alive the memory of the courage and sacrifice of many Ludlow people during the world wars.

Thirteen
People

The six persons who appeared on the popular radio show, Wilfred Pickles' *Have a Go*, which was broadcast from the Town Hall on Tuesday 11 March in 1958, typify the many characters and "lovely people" as Wilfred called them, who have lived in Ludlow down the years. Wilfred stands behind the microphone while his wife Mabel presents a prize to Sally Bodenham (now Stubbs) for winning the jackpot. Wilfred raised a big laugh when he asked Sally, an attractive teenager, if she had "two fern tickets for Whitcliffe"! The other interviewees, from the left, were:

Richard Harding, a retired postmaster, and hereditary freeman of Ludlow, who had returned to live in the town after 47 years with the post office;

Mary Williams, described in the press as "a jovial Ludlovian", who revealed that she had met her husband in a fog at Liverpool, and then sang *Sally* in a manner "that would have done credit to Gracie Fields herself";

John Carter, the Borough Council gardener, who, when asked for his most embarrassing moment, chose the time when the family wedding album was being shown to friends: his son Philip had commented that: "I did not go to that wedding, I stayed with my auntie". In 1992 the same Philip, an old boy of Ludlow Grammar School, would receive the M.B.E. for his work as manager of nursing services for the mentally handicapped at Newcastle-upon-Tyne;

Dorothy Wait, a well known singer, who sang the *Waltz Song* from *Tom Jones;*

Jack Sargent, a gas fitter and Borough Councillor, who announced that he had always wanted to be a parson!

Members of the Bodenham family at the wedding in 1899 between Amy Bodenham, sitting right of centre, and William Bazley (standing next to her), a tea, coffee and provision dealer in the Bull Ring. Amy was a daughter of William and Emma Bodenham. William had come to Ludlow in 1858 and a few years later founded the family firm which is still in business on the corner of King Street and Broad Street. His son, Frederick, not on the picture, later took over the clothing part of the business, which then traded as Frederick J. Bodenham Ltd. Another son of William and Emma, Ernest Bodenham, is standing at the right hand end of the back row. He served on the Borough Council for many years and was Mayor between 1921 and 1923.

Muriel Harvey, daughter of Frederick Bodenham, took over the business after graduating at London University and living in South Wales for some years. As a J.P., churchwarden and Chair of Ludlow Festival and in many other ways, she has given outstanding service to the community.

William Price established a plumbing business in Raven Lane in the 1890s, later moving to Castle Street. This delightful family group, photographed behind their house in Quality Square, shows Bill and his wife Emma with their seven eldest children. Daisy (left) and Gertie (right) stand at the back. The younger children sitting at the front are Dorothy (left), Bill and Doris. The baby on her mother's knee is Winnie (now Winnie Faulkner) while Oswald is held by his father.

One of the family shops at the entrance to Quality Square, 1929. Bill Nicholas, an employee, stands between Doris on the right and Connie (now Faulkner) her younger sister, on the left.

James Vashon, grandson of a Huguenot apothecary, became a surgeon in Ludlow in the early eighteenth century. His son, Rev James Volant Vashon, was Reader of Ludlow from 1739 until 1778. Admiral James Vashon (1742-1828), above left, was his grandson. Entering the navy as a twelve-year-old, he won great glory at the Battle of the Saints in 1782, captaining the ship which broke the enemy line. Sir William Baker (1808-81), above right, was one of the sons of Elizabeth, a niece of Admiral Vashon. He became a distinguished military engineer in India, building canals and railways. His brother James became an admiral. Both Admiral James Vashon and Sir William Baker are featured in the *National Dictionary of Biography*.

One of Sir William Baker's brothers, Vashon Baker, was a naval captain. His daughter, Frances married Robert Twiddy, who farmed at Foldgate in Ludford. Frances is seen here left of the brick porch at Foldgate while Robert Twiddy holds the horse. The child on the horse is Vashon Twiddy, later widely known and respected for his work with the Salvation Army. Three of his children, John Twiddy, Ruth Woolley and Mary Blount and their families still live in Ludlow.

This picture, taken about twenty years ago, shows five generations of the Barker family, well known in the eastern part of Ludlow. George Barker, on the left, and his son, James Barker, standing at the right, were both quarry workers on Clee Hill, but grandson Wesley, standing on the left, became a long distance lorry driver. In front of him is his daughter Susan Morris, who married another lorry driver, and it is her child Jacqueline who is being held by great-great-grandfather George.

Wesley Barker and his wife June, photographed in 1992 with their twenty grandchildren. Wesley has been an outspoken member of the Town Council while June is a part-time assistant at Cliff Stephens, outfitters in Broad Street.

Two of the rich assortment of personalities who have illuminated the history of Ludlow. The country lady (on the left) had a regular produce stall at Ludlow market in the Town Hall. Before leaving for home she always bought her donkey a pint of beer at the George. Harry Preece (right), commonly called Harry Walker, is seen here, unusually well-dressed, in Packer Court. Born in Frog Lane in 1906, Harry was a well-known drover, bringing cattle from Wales to Ludlow market.

Tommy Copper, who lived in Belle Vue Terrace off New Road, was a strict but fair cricket umpire at Burway for many years. Here the Mayor, George Jones, presents him with a bottle of whisky to mark his 94th birthday.

Fourteen

Today and Tomorrow

The recent past has seen a number of exciting projects in Ludlow. This short concluding section features some of the recent developments in Ludlow and looks ahead at schemes still at the planning stage. Together they show that Ludlow remains a community of vision and vitality, even if all its citizens do not share in all these aspirations all the time!

The new livestock market (left) built by McCartneys at The Ox Pasture on the Overton Road, photographed just before it opened for business in February 1995. Ludlow is now the third largest cattle fatstock market in the country, its expansion over recent years owing much to one of its partners, John Uffold (pictured right) who joined the firm in 1981.

Inside the new community sports hall at Ludlow School, opened in February 1995. The project was supported by all three local authorities with much of the capital coming from the sale of surplus playing field land. With this and the smaller sports hall at Ludlow College, also open for use by the public, Ludlow and its district is now at last very well provided with indoor sports facilities.

The link building of the refurbished and enhanced Assembly Rooms, as visualised by an artist. This was to be an almost exact view of how the building looked when it was opened to the public in May 1993. The complex provides for cinema, theatre, lectures, exhibitions and a restaurant, and youth provsion is planned as a second phase. Initiated by the Town Council, the project was masterminded by Ludlow and District Community Association, supported by all three local authorities, by grants and by many individuals and local organisations, In 1994 an independent report rated the facilities among the best in the West Midlands. Though many people played key roles, Councillor Stan Jones (inset) did more than most to start up and sustain the project.

A model illustrating the scheme for enhacing Castle Square, made by John McColgan from a brief prepared by the Town Council and other interested parties, led by Graham Willson Lloyd, Mayor 1993-94. The aim is to make this end of town more attractive in order to sustain its economic and social vitality. Some features of the plan were modified after widespread public consultation, including deletion of the temple-like bandstand, and the project is now being costed by Shropshire County Council, the highways authority. Some local councillors and others would like this to become the completed project which would mark Ludlow's entry into the new millenium.